THE LIFE
AND LEGACY OF POPE
JOHN PAUL II

2

About Wyatt North Publishing

Wyatt North Publishing is a boutique publishing company that always provide high quality, perfectly formatted, Books.

All of our eBooks include a Touch-or-Click Table of Contents, allowing easy and instant access to each section.

We guarantee our Books. If you are not 100% satisfied we will do everything in our power to make you happy. Visit WyattNorth.com for more information. Please feel free to contact us with any questions or comments. We welcome your feedback by email at info@WyattNorth.com.

Foreword

On July 5, Pope Francis approved John Paul for sainthood, saying that Pope John XXIII and John Paul II will be canonized together. The date has not yet been established, although December 8, the Feast of the Immaculate Conception has been suggested. Irrespective of the details, John Paul's canonization appears imminent.

From Poland, John Paul's longtime private secretary, Cardinal Stanislaw Dziwisz, rejoiced at the news. "I thank God that I will live to see the elevation to sainthood the person who I served with love to the last beating of his heart," he stated. Abraham Foxman, as director of the Jewish organization the Anti-Defamation League, received four audiences with Pope John Paul. He spoke for John Paul's numerous supporters when he said, "For many of us Pope John Paul is already a saint, this just formalizes it."

John Paul's pontificate lasted nearly twenty-seven years, one of the longest in papal history. During that time he had an unprecedented amount of contact with the public, including Catholics, non-Catholics, and foreign leaders. He made 104 pastoral visits outside Italy, and 146 within. The Vatican estimates that more than 17.6 million pilgrims participated in his regular Wednesday general audiences alone. He made 38 official visits and met with government leaders on 984 different occasions.

Table of Contents

The Life of Pope John Paul II

The Polish Pope

Nineteen seventy-eight was called the year of three popes. When Cardinal Albino Luciani of Venice was elected to succeed Pope Paul VI, he was applauded for lovingly assuming the name of his two predecessors. That early promise quickly evaporated when the papacy of John Paul I tragically lasted a mere thirty-three days. In that sad context, it was rumored that the College of Cardinals would now seek someone young and vigorous.

When he was elected pope at the age of fifty-eight, Karol Wojtila became the first non-Italian pope in 455 years and the first Slavic pope in history. His election sent a strong message to Communist dictators and affirmed the staunchly Catholic character of Poland.

The papacy of this pope would last an almost unheard-of twenty-seven years. They would be years filled with energy, revitalizing initiatives, and ultimately—controversy.

Formative Years

Karol Jozef Wojtila was born May 18, 1920, to Karol and Emilia
Wojtila. He would be known to family and friends by the nickname,
"Lolek." His elder brother Edmund (known as "Mundek") had been
born a distant fourteen years earlier, while an older sister, Olga, had
lived only a few brief weeks. His father was a noncommissioned
officer in the fledgling Polish army, working in the quartermaster
store. Karol, Sr. had previously served in the Austro-Hungarian
army, and the Jozef in his son's name was probably in honor of the
Emperor Franz Jozef, or alternatively, the Polish leader Jozef
Pilsudsky. Karol Jozef was baptized by a military chaplain at the
parish church of St. Mary's.

The town of Wadowice, where the Wojtila family lived, was nestled
in the foothills of the Carpathian Mountains. It was only thirty miles
from the cultured city of Krakow, which could be reached by train.
Not far was the town of Oswiecim, which in only a few short years
would become infamous under its German name, Auschwitz. During
Karol's formative years, Wadowice held as many as 10,000
residents. Horse-drawn conveyances were the rule, while cars were
still the exception. Nevertheless, as the county seat, Wadowice
boasted government administrative offices, as well as a teacher's
college and a few theaters, including a movie theater. It was also the
site of the army garrison where Karol, Sr. served and which was a
large employer in the area.

Years later, Pope John Paul observed that he had already lost all the people he loved by the time he was twenty. The first to be lost was his mother. Emilia had suffered from heart and kidney problems since childhood. She became increasingly ill and died in 1929 at the age of forty-five, when Karol was not yet nine. This may be the reason that in 1927 Karol, Sr. took early retirement from the military with the rank of captain. (He continued to be known to everyone in town as "Captain.") With the death of Emilia, the rearing of their young son fell entirely to the retired military man. The older Edmund was no longer living at home at the time. Karol's friend, Jerzy Kluger, later recalled how he and Karol played in the Wojtila apartment a good bit after Emilia's death, because the sensitive Karol did not want his father to be alone in his grief. Tragedy struck again when a mere three years after the death of Emilia, Edmund succumbed to scarlet fever. By then a doctor and living in Bielsko, Edmund had been caring for hospital patients during an outbreak of the disease when he contracted it himself and died within days. Edmund was only twenty-six years old.

Karol attended the public high school for boys. The curriculum included Latin and Greek. From his father he also learned German. Thus began his development as a polyglot. Karol was active in a number of extra-curricular activities, including the school's Anti-Aircraft and Gas Weapons Defense League, which was an unfortunate product of the politically troubled 1930s. An outstanding athlete, he excelled as a soccer goalkeeper. Known later as the pope who skied, in his youth he also hiked, swam in the river, and played hockey on frozen ponds. Even as a cardinal, he went kayaking. His deepest passion, however, was acting in youth theater as he came to realize the power of both the written and the spoken word. Upon graduation from high school, he was valedictorian of his class. People who knew him in his youth describe Karol as having been sweet and loving, an attribute they attest he retained throughout his life.

Poland at the time was newly resurgent, having only regained its independence from Austria-Hungary in 1918. Polish nationalism was in the air. Karol's father was strict, but a man of sterling character and integrity, an autodidact who taught his son Polish national pride and an appreciation for Polish literature and the arts. The elder Wojtila would regale Karol and his friend Jerzy with mesmerizing stories about Polish history and its important figures.

When the time came, Karol moved to nearby Krakow with his father to attend Jagiellonian University. They shared a rather dingy basement apartment in a home belonging to the deceased Emilia's two sisters. Jagiellonian University was one of the earliest universities to be established in Europe, with a venerable history dating to 1364. Nicolaus Copernicus was among the important intellects to emerge from there. Karol could not help but feel the weightiness and prestige of this academic environment. In accordance with his growing enthusiasm for the significance of words, he majored in Polish language and literature and began also to study Russian and French. In addition to a rigorous course of study, he continued his theatrical involvement, wrote poetry, and joined various student organizations.

Early Religious Life

The Wojtila's, like many Poles, were devoutly religious. A font of holy water stood outside the apartment to guard their comings and goings. The living room held a well-used prie-dieux with an image of the Black Madonna of Częstochowa before it. Karol often saw his father late at night praying intently before it, and the boy, too, punctuated his day with frequent prayer. Karol went to mass daily before school and served as an altar boy at the church of St. Mary's. During her lifetime, his mother read to him from the New Testament after school. His father took him to a nearby Carmelite monastery, where the monks gave him a scapular of Our Lady of Mount Carmel that he wore throughout his life. (As pope, John Paul would canonize that monastery's best-known monk, Rafal Kalinowsky.) The pilgrimage site of Kalwaria Zebrzydowska (today a UNESCO World Heritage Site) was also nearby, with its series of chapels simulating the distinct paths of Jesus and Mary. Father and son were accustomed to attending the annual passion play there.

Others took note of Karol's exceptional piety. A teacher remarked in his school records on his "special predilection" for the topic of Religion. For two years, he led the Marian Sodality at his school, thus beginning his lifelong devotion to the Holy Mother. On one terrible occasion, the school custodian was fatally hit by a car right in front of the school. Out of an entire school of horrified onlookers, it was Karol, the altar boy, who thought to run for the priest to administer last rights. Nevertheless, while many acquaintances envisioned a vocation for him, Karol at that time saw a future devoted to literature and the theater.

Karol Wojtila and the Jews, the First Chapter

Although the Jewish presence in Poland would be virtually obliterated in W.W.II, Jews in pre-war Poland were a very sizable and important minority. They were thoroughly incorporated into Polish society, having been present in Poland since at least as early as the 10th century. The town of Wadowice, however, was a bit more ethnically uniform. By the start of W.W.II, Jews comprised only an estimated 10–20 percent of the population, substantially lower than in other parts of Poland. Nevertheless, Jews formed the second-largest demographic segment in Wadowice. They were principally artisans and shopkeepers; some were professionals.

Accordingly, young Karol grew up sharing life with his Jewish neighbors. Karol's elementary school class was at least one-fourth Jewish. The Wojtila family lived in a modest but middle-class three-room apartment, which was rented from a Jewish landlord. The landlord's glass goods shop was located at street level, and another Jewish family, the Beers, also lived within the building. Karol had Jewish friends and sometimes substituted on the Jewish soccer team when their goalkeeper wasn't available. Among his very best friends while growing up was Jerzy ("Jorek") Kluger, whose attorney father was the elected head of Wadowice's Jewish community and had been an officer with Pilsudsky's legions. "Jorek" and "Lolek" played "Cowboys and Indians" together and remained close throughout their school years. In one instance, Karol and his father, at the invitation of Jerzy's father, attended a synagogue cantorial performance by a renowned young Jewish soldier who was stationed in the local garrison. A number of other Christian notables in the community attended that performance as well.

Later, when the teenaged Karol became active in youth theater, one of his frequent leading ladies was his neighbor, the beautiful Regina ("Ginka") Beers, with whom he shared romantic scenes. In addition, Father Leonard Prowchownik, who decried Poland's Nazi-inspired economic boycott of Jews, became pastor at St. Mary's and was highly influential in maintaining an atmosphere of tolerance in the town. Father Prowchownik and Jerzy's grandmother could often be seen walking together and holding lively discussions. (Since both were deaf, the discussions were also loud.) These and other experiences would drive Karol's later decisions as pope to build bridges with the Jewish community.

The Darkening Sky

Hitler came to power in Germany at the beginning of 1933, and the Nazi boycott of Jewish businesses followed soon after. The Nuremberg Laws depriving Jews of German citizenship and instituting other draconian restrictions were introduced in 1935. Across the border in Poland, instability was growing even before the two Karols left Wadowice for Krakow. The great Polish hero Jozef Pilsudski had held a tolerant position toward Poland's ethnic minorities. When he died in 1935, the floodgates of anti-Semitism opened, fanned by what was happening in nearby Germany. One of those inciting hatred was Cardinal Augustin Hlond, the primate of Poland, who used a pastoral letter to launch a vituperative attack against Jews in general and Polish Jews in particular.

Within Wadowice, however, Father Prowchownik had a more direct impact, and he was counseling that anti-Semitism was anti-Christian. Even so, there were outbursts of anti-Semitism in Wadowice during Karol's senior year of high school. After a particularly bad incident, the normally reserved Captain Wojtila took pains to send warm regards to Jerzy's father, thus making clear his own opposition to the nastiness that had occurred.

The Wojtila's friend and neighbor, young Ginka Beers was an aspiring physician and two years older than Karol. Feeling the press of anti-Semitism during a brief, unpleasant stint at Jagiellonian University, she decided to try her luck in British Mandate Palestine. Both Karols were profoundly disturbed by her leaving. The elder

Karol plaintively reminded her that not all Poles were anti-Semitic. The younger Karol became red-faced and teary-eyed and was too upset to speak. By leaving when she did, Ginka would escape the Holocaust, but her parents and sister would perish.

Jerzy Kluger was experiencing similar problems. He left his engineering studies in Warsaw after only one month because of increasingly violent anti-Semitism. Having repeatedly refused to sit in the back of the classroom, he was viciously beaten several times. When his father visited Warsaw and discovered Jerzy's badly bruised face, he forced him to return home to Wadowice.

For his part, Karol began his university studies in the fall of 1938. Due to the ominous militarization of Germany, he had to take part in compulsory Polish military training both before and after his first year of university, but he was exempted from regular military service because of his studies. Thus, he was in Krakow preparing for the new school year when on September 1, 1939, the first air raid sirens sounded the German invasion of Poland and the beginning of World War II. He assisted with Mass at the Wawel Cathedral, as was his custom on the first Friday of the month, and then hurried home to his father. They joined the flood of refugees fleeing eastward. Dodging the strafing German planes that killed many tens of thousands fleeing on foot like themselves, they advanced about one hundred miles, only to hear that the Russians were now invading from the east.

There had long been enmity between Poles and Russians. Many Poles now feared the godlessness of the Soviets even more than the brutality of the Germans. The elder Wojtila was exhausted. Father and son decided to return to Krakow.

The Nazi plan for Poland was to create *Lebensraum*—"living space"—for ethnic Germans. Their short-term plan for the Polish people was to reduce the population to manageable numbers and employ the survivors as slave laborers. Depopulation of the territory would take place, in part, through long-term starvation. Poles were expected to subsist on a diet so minimal that it weakened resistance to disease, and food became largely unavailable to them. (Two years later, the Nazi governor Hans Frank would estimate that the majority of Poles were consuming only 600 calories per day.) Poles would be kept uneducated, unaware, and hence unable to mount an organized resistance. In order to accomplish that aim, the Polish intelligentsia had to be liquidated, and all residue of Polish national identity had to be obliterated.

On a single day in November 1939, 183 students, professors, and other staff of Jagiellonian University were arrested and deported to the Sachsenhausen Concentration Camp. The university was closed, along with all other institutions of secondary and higher education in Poland. At least thirty-four professors and other staff of the university would be killed in the course of the war, either in concentration camps or by the Soviets.

In this setting, any act of Polish cultural resistance was heroic and accomplished at the risk of one's own life and the lives of others. And that is precisely where we locate Karol Wojtila, who became one of approximately 800 students studying clandestinely when the university took its operations underground. He was also deeply involved in keeping Polish theater alive. The performances took place before small groups of people in private apartments. Karol even wrote several plays based on Old Testament topics but inspired by the Nazi oppression. In addition, he translated Sophocles' *Oedipus* from Greek into Polish. All such activities had to be undertaken between work time and curfew. Going out after curfew meant being shot. Being caught at what they were doing would also have meant being shot.

Beatings, shootings, and roundups were part of everyday life. With the university officially closed, it was necessary for Karol to obtain a work permit in order to remain in Krakow without being deported to a forced labor camp or executed. Initially he was able to work as a messenger, but after a time he was forced into manual labor for the Solvay chemical company. For an entire bitter winter, he shoveled limestone outdoors in a quarry. Those who knew him then say he responded to the unaccustomed work stoically, quietly.

He was engaged in this harsh manual labor for only a few months. In the spring, he became the assistant of the quarry's blaster. The following fall, in 1941, he was transferred to a different site, the Solvay factory's water purification unit. There, he received additional food, since the plant fed the workers soup with a bit of bread. Working the night shift, he was able to sneak time to read. One of the books he read at that time held the writings of St. Louis Grignon de Montfort, from whom he learned that true Marian piety was focused on Christ, since Mary, properly understood, was the first disciple of Christ. At the same time, Karol also received an unexpected education in the life of a common laborer, which would later make him a better pastor.

The parish where he lived was struggling. Most of the priests had been arrested. As a result, the remaining priests turned to lay leaders for help, most notably Jan Tyranowski, who established a "Living Rosary," comprised of groups of young men committed to prayer and spiritual growth. Each group had its own leader, and Karol was one of the earliest group leaders. The groups, of course, had to meet secretly. In addition, the group leaders met with Tyranowski for study, training, and guidance. In Jan Tyranowski, Karol found both a teacher and a role model. From the personal example of Tyranowski, he learned that lay people, not only priests, could be vessels for the holy in their daily lives. He took to heart an idea he heard from Tyranowski: it is not hard to be a saint. Very importantly, Tyranowski introduced him to the works of the Spanish mystic,

Saint John of the Cross, who taught that God could only be reached by complete self-surrender.

During this time, some of Karol's friends were involved in more activist types of resistance. Some were armed. Others helped save Jews by supplying them with false baptismal certificates to pass as Christians. Karol Wojtila never claimed to have saved any Jewish lives during the war. He said that he could not claim what he did not do. He provided what assistance he could to Poles whose family members had been arrested. In one case he showed up at work without a jacket because he had given his to a man without one. And he continued to believe in the power of prayer—so he prayed.

The Vocation

Captain Wojtila had taken to his bed shortly after Christmastime 1940. On a bitterly cold day in February 1941, Karol returned home from work to find his father dead, the blankets in which he was wrapped still warm. Even many years later, he confessed to being troubled that his father had died alone. He admitted that he was never so lonely as during the period after his father's death. Some friends convinced him to come live with them for a time because they were worried about him.

Karol was twenty years old and an orphan. As difficult as this time was for him, it was now that his vocation began to come into focus. The trials and the joys of his life had coalesced to lead him to the priesthood. He contemplated this course for a while and then, in the fall of 1942, submitted himself at the archbishop's residence as a candidate for the priesthood.

It was not a safe path to tread. Some students had already been executed, others sent to Auschwitz. The seminary had gone underground. Karol studied in secret while continuing to work for Solvay and perform in the clandestine theater. He was not to tell anyone what he was doing. Eventually, it became necessary to share the information with his theater friends, some of whom tried to change his mind.

When danger did come, it was not in the form expected. In February 1944, Karol was walking home from work in the factory when he was struck unconscious by a German truck. He experienced a severe concussion, cuts and bruises, and a shoulder injury. He awoke in the hospital with a bandaged head and his arm in a cast, and he remained in the hospital for the next two weeks. Did this head injury play a role in his later Parkinson's disease? Perhaps one day, science will clarify the possible links. For his part, Karol considered his survival an act of grace.

The Polish Warsaw Uprising began on August 1, 1944. To prevent a similar occurrence in Krakow, the Nazis began rounding up young men. Karol was actually hiding in his apartment when the house where he lived was searched by the Gestapo. Under the circumstances, the archbishop called his seminarians to take refuge within his residence. Studies now took place on a full-time schedule within those confines.

On January 17–18, 1945, the Nazis retreated from Krakow. One oppressive regime was replaced by another. The Soviet Union was now in control, and they installed a communist government. Karol continued his theological studies at the newly reopened Jagiellonian University and graduated in 1946. The archbishop, who by now had been named a cardinal, wanted Karol to continue his studies in Rome, so Karol's installation as sub-deacon, deacon, and then priest followed in swift succession during the summer and fall of 1946. He left for Rome in mid-November 1946, traveling by train to Paris and then on to Rome. It was Father Wojtila's first time outside of Poland.

Life as a Priest

Father Wojtila lived with other priests and seminarians in the Belgian College while studying at the Pontifical Athenaeum of St Thomas Aquinas. The international climate suited him. He was able to practice his French and German and began also to study Italian and English. He toured Rome and the Italian countryside with his colleagues, learning about the history of the Church through its historical sites. It was during this time that he made a visit San Giovanni Rotondo to see the famed stigmatist Padre Pio, whom he would later raise to sainthood. Like others, he was most impressed with Padre Pio's evident suffering while celebrating Mass. In the summer, Father Wojtila was able to tour Europe to see firsthand how Catholicism was expressed in different locations. He made a pilgrimage to the Sanctuary of Ars (France), where St John Mary Vianney, the Curé of Ars and patron saint of priests, resided. He came away committed to reaching out to laypeople through the confessional, as the Curé had done. This would become a focal point of his pastoral mission.

He completed his doctoral dissertation, which was written in Latin, on *The Doctrine of Faith According to St. John of the Cross* and completed his doctorate with near-perfect marks. He did not, however, receive his degree from the Pontifical Athenaeum because he didn't have the money to publish his dissertation, which was the final prerequisite. When he returned to Poland, he submitted the dissertation to Jagiellonian University and received his doctoral degree there at the end of 1948.

No longer a student, Father Wojtila was assigned to his first parish as an assistant cleric in a small, rural town called Niegowi, located in the foothills of the Carpathian Mountains not far from Krakow. He would remain there for eight months, educating children, conducting marriages and baptisms, hearing confession, and actively working to engage the people of his parish. He even started a drama club and directed a play.

In 1949, he was transferred back to Krakow, to a large parish consisting of many intellectuals. At St. Florian's, Father Wojtila was expected to interact not only with the regular members of the parish, but also with students from Jagiellonian University, Krakow Polytechnic, and the Academy of Fine Arts, serving as a kind of university chaplain. He held lectures, organized study groups, and visited dormitories. Under the influence of the liturgical renewal movement, he began a student choir and taught them to sing various parts of the Mass in Gregorian chant. He again directed plays, and in 1950, he started an innovative marriage preparation program, which enabled him to interact with burgeoning families. The range of his evangelism also encompassed country hikes, skiing, and kayaking. He was dedicated to bringing Catholicism out into the world.

He began to write essays for Catholic publications. Employing pseudonyms, he wrote plays exploring religious and philosophical themes. He also wrote poetry. The number of his followers grew as his reputation spread. He was known for openness, kindness, and an exacting level of intellectualism. He also impressed people with his devotion to a life of poverty, for his garments were invariably threadbare, and he gave away any presents bestowed upon him to whomever he deemed more needful. Even other priests respected him for his obviously genuine piety and goodness.

In Communist Poland, it was still important to be circumspect about Catholic undertakings. Informers were always listening for anyone speaking against the regime. Catholic youth groups had been officially banned. Restrictions on the Catholic Church were onerous and variable. As a result, many activities had to be conducted carefully. Not everyone with whom Father Wojtila interacted knew or wanted to know the young priest's real name. Some knew him as "Wujek," (Uncle), while others called him "Sadok." The clever priest took these designations from his knowledge of literature and drama.

In 1951, Father Wojtila left the parish to study for a second doctorate in philosophy, but his pastoral mission persisted as he continued to minister to his sizable following. He received his second doctorate from Jagiellonian University at the beginning of 1954, writing on the topic: *An Evaluation of the Possibility of Constructing a Christian Ethics on the Basis of the System of Max Scheler.* In October of that year, he joined the Philosophy Department at the Catholic University of Lublin, the only Catholic university allowed to exist, albeit with difficulty, within the Communist orbit. In 1956, he was named to the Chair of Ethics, which he held for over twenty years. He donated his salary to student scholarship funds and continued his subsistence lifestyle. Because he commuted to Lublin from Krakow, he was able to maintain his chaplaincy in Krakow. He was also a chaplain, of sorts, to the students in Lublin, always available to speak with them or hear their confessions. Some of his best-attended courses were in Ethics, where he championed self-giving and coexistence as the keys to fulfillment.

In 1960, he published his first book, *Love and Responsibility*, a treatment of sexual and marital ethics drawn both from his philosophical pursuits and his pastoral mission. In it, he celebrated sex within the vocation of marriage. This was a rather more positive view of sexual expression than was usually found in Church discussions. He was expressing his views in the general context of the sexual revolution and the particular situation in Communist Poland. In order to undermine the Church, Poland's Communist government encouraged sexual license among young people and had passed an abortion law permitting it as a birth control option. Instead, Father Wojtila argued that sexuality should *not* involve the primacy of self, but rather the mutuality of relationship. Accordingly, sexuality should be treated *not* as an expression of personal autonomy, but rather of personal responsibility for another person.

Just before Pope Pius XII passed away, he named the young priest a bishop (1958), making the thirty-eight-year-old Wojtila the youngest bishop in Poland. In due course, he would be named an archbishop (1964) and finally a cardinal (1967).

Karol Wojtila's Role in Vatican II

The Second Vatican Council, or Vatican II as it was dubbed, was convened by Pope John XXIII in October 1962. He would not live to see its conclusion, and its agenda would be carried forward by Pope Paul VI. This ecumenical council took place over four autumns. Its goal was to renew the Church and enable it to speak in the modern world. It also aimed to create unity within the growing diversity of the universal Church.

At its beginning, Wojtila was a bishop, but he would soon be named Archbishop of Krakow. He was present at all four annual sessions, and it was his first time outside of Poland since he had left his studies in Rome. He took advantage of his leave-taking from Poland to also make an inspirational visit to Egypt, Israel, and the Jordanian-occupied territories, as Pope Pius VI had suggested Council participants do.

Bishop Wojtila found the Council profoundly spiritual, and he relished the vitality of the theological discourse over issues. The breadth of racial and cultural diversity he found among the clergy delighted him. He fully believed that the Holy Spirit was guiding the progress of the Council, and he was prepared to aid in the Council's efforts to chart a course for the new millennium. Toward that end, he spoke before the Council multiple times each year. The importance of addressing the human condition and the role of the laity were recurring themes in his learned speeches (known in the Council's terminology as "interventions").

His best-known contributions had to do with formulating and expressing the role of the Church in the modern world. He helped write the Pastoral Constitution on the Church in the Modern World, *Gaudium et Spes* ("Joy and Hope"), which was one of four Apostolic Constitutions resulting from Vatican II and promulgated by Pope Paul VI in December 1965.

By the end of Vatican II, Archbishop Wojtila's reputation would no longer be confined to Poland. He was now well-known to his fellow clergy throughout the world.

Back in Poland

Archbishop Wojtila's second book came about as a result of his participation in the Council. *Person and Act* was an attempt to express the philosophical underpinnings of the teachings that emerged from Vatican II. The book is notoriously difficult reading. An English edition exists, but critics argue that it has been modified from the original so that it does not always represent the author's thinking.

One of the vital documents from Vatican II was *Dignitatis Humanae*, which among its other teachings declared that people have a right to religious freedom, both freedom from coercion to worship and freedom to worship according to their conscience. The document encouraged the structuring of society to ensure that right. This pronouncement created an obvious problem for the Communist government in Poland, whose goal was to control and suppress the Church in Poland. Then, too, both the Church in Poland and the Communist government in Poland lived under the cloud of potential Soviet intervention, which neither group wanted. Consequently, both were engaged in a delicate balancing act.

The Communist government in Poland asserted a great deal of control over Church activities, including the right to veto appointments. When that government pressed for the nomination of Karol Wojtila to become Archbishop of Krakow, they no doubt saw him as an inexperienced young man who was unschooled in politics and would be easy to manipulate. What they got was more than they bargained for. Throughout his clerical career in Poland, he confounded the regime.

Were Catholic charities banned? He created less formal charitable networks at the parish level. Was there a moratorium on creating new parishes? He found ways to evangelize the population of the neighborhood to create the reality of a parish. Did the communist bureaucrats refuse to process permits for building new churches? He created a groundswell of support that caused problems for the government and got the church built.

The regime had its victories, too, as when Father Jozef Kurzeja, who had been agitating for the building of a church in a particular location, was so hounded by the security police that he died of heart failure at the youthful age of thirty-nine. Archbishop Wojtila saw to it that the church was built. He was able to dedicate it as pope, seven years after Father Kurzeja's death, in 1983.

In a Communist country, the dominant relationship was between the state and the individual, and the individual was clearly the subordinate. The individual's loyalty had to be to the state. All other counter-loyalties were in the way, including the bonds of family and community. Archbishop Wojtila's strength was in building community, and he created ties among all its facets: young marrieds, youth, elderly, infirm and disabled, laity, clergy, and uncommitted. He also extended an ecumenical hand in friendship to the tiny

Protestant minority in Krakow. The archbishop's success in forging ties flew in the face of Communist goals. As a result, his movements were increasingly monitored, and his residence was bugged. Occasionally, there was even cloak-and-dagger intrigue: the secret police following Wojtila's car were eluded through fancy driving maneuvers and a quick change of vehicles.

In all his efforts, Archbishop Wojtila strove to implement the ideals of human dignity that emerged from Vatican II, but there were two areas in particular where Vatican II became his focus. First, his next book, *Sources of Renewal* (published in 1970), was a guide to the documents of Vatican II. Second, he organized a Synod of Krakow, in which he recreated for the clergy and laity of his jurisdiction the experience of Vatican II. Whereas a Synod would normally deal with issues of canon law, this Synod would focus on pastoral issues. The chief question asked of the participants was how the guidelines of Vatican II could be implemented within their diocese. Throughout the duration of the Synod, which lasted through most of the 1970s, tens of thousands of Catholics in Krakow were engaging with the documents of Vatican II and debating how to realize them in their lives. The archbishop's book provided a commentary to the texts with which they grappled. The outcome of the process was an educated laity that functioned as a community and had created their own stake in how Vatican II and Catholicism worked within their churches and within their lives. The Synod was a master stroke of pastoral and administrative management.

When Pope Paul VI named him a cardinal in 1967, Cardinal Wojtila developed even more outlets for his talents, and his reputation and status grew accordingly. The Polish government usually granted him permission to travel, unlike some of his Polish colleagues. He traveled frequently to Rome for meetings of the congregations in which he served, and he became active on the Synod of Bishops, which met annually to discuss important issues. In 1969 he traveled for a month to Polish communities throughout Canada and the United States. In 1973, he traveled to Australia for the International Eucharistic Congress, at which time he also visited the Philippines, New Guinea, and New Zealand. There were other trips as well, including a return tour of the United States.

In 1976, only two years before his death, Pope Paul VI invited Cardinal Wojtila to conduct the annual Lenten retreat for himself and the Roman Curia. Cardinal Wojtila was to present a series of twenty-two lectures before the assemblage. It was a singular honor, and it put the cardinal on view before a host of very influential figures.

The Year With Three Popes

In August of 1978, the aged Pope Paul died. Within the same month, Cardinal Albino Luciani of Venice was elected pope in his stead. The new pope sought to honor his two great predecessors, John XXIII and Paul VI, by taking both their names. The unique choice of a double name endeared him the populace, both for the humility it demonstrated (his motto was *humilitas*) and because the choice contained the reassurance of continuity. But then, the world was dismayed when only thirty-three days later Pope John Paul I suddenly passed away. On October 16, 1978, on the second day of deliberations and the eighth ballot, Karol Wojtyla, the Cardinal Archbishop of Krakow, was elected pope.

It was not an outcome that Cardinal Wojtila had wanted. Friends who saw him before he left Poland for John Paul I's funeral in Rome have indicated he may have had an intuition or a premonition that this would occur. His goodbyes seemed too serious, too somber. Becoming pope would mean leaving behind forever a lifetime of friendships and connections, the cultural and intellectual stimulation of his academic circle, and the city and country that he loved. He accepted the decision, as he put it, with obedience to Christ.

In one respect, the choice of Wojtila made sense to all who heard: this man was young and in good health. His election, in that respect at least, seemed a reaction to the stunning loss that had just occurred. But there were other aspects to Wojtyla's election that came as a complete surprise. Upon hearing the unfamiliar sound of his name, some listeners thought he was African. "Who is he?" the people congregating in St. Peter's Square wanted to know.

The content of the conclave's deliberations was, of course, confidential, but this is what most experts believe occurred: It seems a deadlock had arisen between two popular Italian choices. Unable to find another suitable Italian candidate, the cardinals began to look farther afield. The Church at the time was experiencing discord, partially due to difficulty in implementing Vatican II and partially due to the general moral malaise of modern culture. Cardinal Wojtila was known to have successfully negotiated this challenging course within his own diocese. Moreover, he had managed to do it behind the Iron Curtain. If he had shortcomings as an administrator, he was a brilliant pastor. In addition, his star had been steadily rising among his fellow bishops.

And so Karol Wojtila became the first non-Italian pope in 455 years, and the first Slavic pope in history. Catholic Poland, especially, rejoiced.

After twenty years as bishop, fourteen of them as the successful leader of a major metropolitan cultural center under extraordinarily challenging circumstances, the cardinal felt thoroughly comfortable with his new role as pope. He was confident that if the Holy Spirit had led him here, he must have the attributes that were needed for the job. From the beginning, he signaled to the Roman Curia that things were going to change: they would not control him. He broke with the etiquette of precedence at every turn, always doing things his way. If this made the Curia nervous, Pope John Paul II was not overly troubled by it. His management style as bishop had always been to pursue and accomplish his goals. The bureaucracy could take care of itself. When Pope John XXIII had called for a Second Vatican Council, he famously declared that it was time to open the windows of the Vatican to let in fresh air. Now, Pope John Paul opened the doors as well.

While the world celebrated the new pope, or at least waited to see what it would all mean, the Communist regime in Poland was horrified. Karol Wojtila had long been a thorn in their side, and he quickly made it clear that relocation wouldn't alter his outspokenness. The new pope made frequent references to oppressed churches, the lack of liberty in some parts of the world, and the need for religious freedom in all societies. What's more, he was able to address the various nationalities comprising the Soviet Union and its orbit in their own languages. Not just Catholic Poland was at stake, but also heavily Catholic Lithuania, the Ukraine, Belorussia, and Czechoslovakia. (As archbishop, Wojtila had already been engaged in the clandestine ordination of Czechoslovak priests.) The Soviet Union made it clear to Poland that it wasn't amused by this Polish export. The KGB opened a dossier. Changes were indeed coming.

Pope John Paul's Vision for the Church

As pope, John Paul looked to the words of Jesus to Peter, his predecessor, for guidance: "And when you have turned again, strengthen your brethren" (Luke 22:32). Toward that end, John Paul's first and ongoing efforts were to strengthen the members of the Church.

One of his first aims was to strengthen the family. Towards that end, at the beginning of his papacy, he organized his Wednesday general audiences into a series of 129 lectures organized around a single theme. This took place between September 1979 and November 1984. These homilies were later compiled and published as *The Theology of the Body*, which was, in part, an extended attempt to purge any residue of Gnostic distain for the human body. In these talks, he presented very carefully his view of family relations, elaborating what he had said earlier in his book, *Love and Responsibility*. Marriage was a vocation, just as the priesthood was a vocation, and fidelity was the core of both.

He included his explanation for why natural sexual relations, unimpeded by unnatural birth control interventions, was God's plan to uphold the human dignity of husband and wife. While he conceded that family planning was part of a responsible relationship, he argued that this could only take place through Church-approved, natural means of fertility regulation. Artificial means of birth control were, he argued, dehumanizing.

Another early focus was the priesthood. In 1979, on Holy Thursday (April 8), the day when priests renew their vows, he addressed a letter to every Catholic priest. The salutation read: "My Dear Brother Priests." His message was designed to reinvigorate their commitment to their vocations and to restore lost morale. Whereas Pope Paul had allowed more than 32,000 priests to be released from their vows, John Paul was going to make the process harder. He wanted his priests to recall why they had become priests and to recover that sense of purpose. He reminded them of the importance of their priestly celibacy, which is a gift of the Spirit, a renunciation for the sake of the kingdom of heaven. Through this renunciation, the priest becomes a man serving others and is thereby able to build up the Church.

As is well-known, the new pope very soon went traveling. He traveled more extensively than any pope before, going personally to speak with the faithful and encourage them. With targeted visits to Africa and Asia, he demonstrated the importance of youthful churches for the future. And while in Africa, he deflected criticism about his many trips by suggesting that popes should take their cues not just from St. Peter but also from the peripatetic St. Paul. He didn't only speak to Catholics, however. One of his earliest trips brought him before the United Nations (October 1979), where in an hour-long address to the General Assembly, he lectured the nations of the world on human rights and human freedom.

Karol Wojtila had always believed the Church's core task was to proclaim God's love, mercy, and forgiveness. This was his vision as he assumed leadership of the Church, and he articulated it in his first three encyclicals as pope. He saw this as a joyous message and one that elevated the dignity of all human beings.

He knew very well that it was his task as pope to complete the implementation of Vatican II. Accordingly, he consistently looked to the Second Vatican Council for direction, particularly the conciliar statements on ecumenism, religious freedom, and the laity. He especially focused on *Gaudium et Spes* (see above) with its emphasis on the role of the church in the modern world, the dignity of the human person, and the community of mankind. The Church didn't need to be confined to church buildings; it had a role to play out and about in the modern world.

While Vatican II had begun the process of "declericalization," or adjusting the unbalanced emphasis on the clergy, it was John Paul who gave impetus to the effort. He wanted reemphasis on the Church as a community in which all the baptized are equally important. As such, there was room for a multiplicity of voices—women, young people, and various Catholic movements—to be heard within the overarching unity of the Trinity. The Trinity itself was the model for unity in diversity, and it was the foundation for John Paul's renewal efforts for the Church.

Latin America

John Paul's first foray as pope into the world of diplomacy occurred very shortly after his election. In December 1978, he offered the Vatican's services (not his personal services, however) as mediator in a border dispute between Chile and Argentina that threatened to erupt into war. The Vatican hadn't been involved in a mediation of this sort since 1885, and some were afraid that failure would diminish the Vatican's prestige. For his part, John Paul felt that he could not stand aside while two Catholic countries teetered on the brink. The initiative, however, succeeded.

The following month came John Paul's first trip abroad as pope. It would be to Mexico. Latin America holds nearly half of the world's Catholics. In targeting Mexico for his first pilgrimage, he signaled the importance of Latin America within the Catholic world. It was an acknowledgement welcomed by the Mexican people. It is estimated that a million Mexicans lined the short route from the airport into Mexico City. Their enthusiasm was matched at every point of the pope's trip. In a talk before a half-million indigenous people from Oaxaca and Chiapas, he spoke of the injustices perpetrated against them, the need for recognition of their dignity, and the imperative for bold social change.

During that first trip to Mexico, he addressed an important conference of Latin American bishops, the general assembly of CELAM. His goal in speaking to them was to establish how the Church should function at that time and in that place. The history of the Catholic Church in Latin America has not always been a happy one. The Church has tended to align itself with the sources of power and the causes of oppression. Rejecting that history, activist priests had recently arisen, sometimes espousing violent expressions of liberation theology that had been shaped by Marxism. The Mexican government itself represented a reaction against the Church. It was secular, anti-clerical, and did not have formal relations with the Vatican. In that context, John Paul spoke pointedly of the need to emphasize social justice, but he also tried to steer his more radical listeners back to a course of doctrinal orthodoxy. It was his opening volley in a battle against the infiltration of what he perceived as Marxist ideas into Church life. As one who had lived a good part of his life in the shadow of Marxist ideology, he knew that it could not be reconciled with Catholic principles.

His positions would be spelled out more thoroughly in the encyclicals and teachings that followed that first visit.

John Paul's focus on Latin America was unwavering, although some would argue it was heavy-handed. In the years that followed, he disciplined priests who became too embroiled in partisan politics, such as several who held posts in the Marxist-influenced Sandinista government of Nicaragua. He went as far as to assume control of the appointment of officers of the Confederation of Latin American Religious to prevent extremists from assuming leadership of the organization. The Peruvian priest who had coined the term "liberation theology," Father Gustavo Gutierrez, was required to revise some of his writings. The Brazilian theologian Leonardo Boff, who was outspoken in his criticism of, among other things, the Church hierarchical structure, left the priesthood when he was on the verge of being silenced for the second time.

Nevertheless, during his 1987 trip to Chile while it was under the Pinochet dictatorship, John Paul said Mass for a huge audience and provided a forum for a series of speakers describing political censorship, torture, and murder. His trip is considered a turning point in Chile's transition to democracy.

It was during the pontificate of John Paul, that Oscar Romero, Archbishop of San Salvador, was horribly murdered while celebrating mass. Only days before his death in March 1980 he had said, "You can tell the people that if they succeed in killing me, that I forgive and bless those who do it. Hopefully, they will realize they are wasting their time. A bishop will die, but the Church of God, which is the people, will never perish." Of course Romero was only the most senior of the Church figures at risk in El Salvador for working with the poor. December 1980 saw the murder of the four American churchwomen, but there were many others as well.

In 1997, a cause was opened for Romero, and John Paul bestowed upon him the title of Servant of God, the first of the four stages of canonization. Shortly before the death of John Paul, an official announced that Romero's beatification was about to proceed, but under Pope Benedict canonizations slowed, and the beatification did not occur. It is possible that the cause has not progressed because of a (rightly or wrongly) perceived alignment of Romero with Liberation Theology. In 2013, the same official announced that the process had been "unblocked" by Pope Francis.

With his emphasis on social justice and inclusiveness, John Paul criticized human rights violations in military governments, called for solidarity with the poor, and canonized Juan Diego (a 16th century indigenous person who saw a vision of Mary as Our Lady of Guadalupe). John Paul made a trip to somewhere in Latin America nearly every year of his papacy, the last when he was 82.

Religious Freedom

Although he took oblique slaps at Communism from the beginning of his pontificate, making frequent reference to religious freedom, John Paul's first encyclical of March 1979 held a more frontal assault. *Redemptor Hominis* (The Redeemer of Man) refers to the "totalitarianisms of this century." It is clear that he did not only mean Nazism. The document refers to states where power is imposed by a particular group upon all other members of the society. Since the duty of the state is to serve the common good, all citizens must be assured their rights.

There is a type of atheism, the text continues, that is structured as a society. Yet a society that grants only atheism the right of citizenship and deprives religious believers of rights is unacceptable. The curtailment of religious freedom—regardless of the religion involved—is an assault on human dignity. The role of the Church, on the other hand, is to be a guardian of freedom. *Redemptor Hominis* goes on to allude to reasons for not going into full detail but requests of pertinent officials that they respect the right of religious freedom and enable the Church to conduct its activities. Nowhere does the letter call Communism by name, but the intent is clear. It should be noted that *Redemptor Hominis* criticizes not just Communism, but also unbridled capitalism and consumerism.

In 1966, the Polish government had refused a disappointed Pope Paul VI entry into Poland for the series of celebrations marking one thousand years of Christianity in Poland. Now, in 1979, the country was about to celebrate the nine-hundred-year anniversary of the martyrdom of St. Stanislaus, the first bishop of Krakow. The event had the potential to become an anti-government forum because Stanislaus was known for speaking up against power. The former Archbishop of Krakow had made it clear that he wanted to be present both for that celebration and for the closing of the Synod of Krakow he had initiated. The government knew it was facing a different situation than in 1966, and it feared public reaction against an outright rejection of the request. Instead, a delay in the visit was negotiated. The pope could come after the celebrations for St. Stanislaus were concluded.

The Communist victory was fleeting. The Polish episcopate simply extended the closing date of both celebrations until the pope could come to participate in them.

When a Polish pope was first named, the Polish government had tried to put a positive spin on the situation by invoking Polish nationalism. On the occasion of the pope's return, it was all the Communists could do to stay out of the way. They helped very little with the overwhelming task of preparing for the pope's visit. Preparations, including measures to safely control the large crowds anticipated, were organized at a grass-roots level by common people, both believers and non-believers, sometimes under the guidance of Polish clerics but sometimes organized by the people themselves.

In June 1979, Karol Wojtila returned to Poland as Pope John Paul II. One million Poles turned out at the start of his visit for an outdoor Mass conducted in Victory Square (now Pilsudsky Square) in the center of Warsaw. That number would only grow as the pope moved throughout Poland on his itinerary. Millions more followed on radio and television. The theme of John Paul's sermon in Victory Square was Christ's central place in Polish history. Anyone who opposed this truth of Polish history harmed the Polish people. He affirmed that Christ would continue to hold pride of place in the future. He offered to God Poland's history of suffering, and he included in that history the Jews who had died in the Warsaw ghetto "in their hundreds of thousands." As he spoke, the people chanted: we want God, we want God in schools, we want God in the family, we want God…

Throughout the nine days of his visit, John Paul continued to hammer the message that Polish history and the Polish heart could only be understood through its Catholic shrines and Catholic devotion. Toward the end of his stay in Krakow, a vast gathering of young people threatened to erupt into a massive anti-government demonstration, perhaps even a riot. Sensing the danger and not wanting to encourage a possible tragedy, the pope put aside his planned remarks and instead bantered gently with the crowd. Speaking extemporaneously, he was able to calm the situation.

By the end of his visit, an estimated thirteen million Poles had seen the pope in person. Heartened and renewed by his words, they gained a sense of their own numbers, unity, and worth.

The Communist governments of Europe had cause to worry. The pope had galvanized Poland's population. He had called Poles to authentic living and asked audiences comprised of both believers and nonbelievers whether they had the maturity to be nonconformists. Many observers credit the pope's visit with the emergence of the non-violent labor movement, Solidarity, which arose at the Lenin Shipyard in Gdansk (also known as the Gdansk Shipyard) under the leadership of an unemployed electrician, Lech Walesa, who had been fired from his position at the shipyard in 1976 due to his activism. On August 14, 1980, seventeen thousand workers seized control of the Lenin Shipyard to protest rising prices and other issues. Workers in twenty nearby factories joined the strike.

Walesa affirmed that the pope had made them aware of their numerical strength and told them not to be afraid. Poles had reason to be afraid: a 1970 worker protest had ended with dozens killed and more than one thousand wounded from machine-gun fire, and both the 1956 Hungarian Uprising and the 1968 Prague Spring had been silenced when Soviet tanks rolled in.

Yet less than a year after the pope's visit, the Communist regime would be forced to authorize the existence of this first independent, non-Communist trade union, which occurred on August 31, 1980. By 1981, Solidarity's membership was more than nine million, one-third of Polish workers. Solidarity was suppressed through much of the 1980s under martial law imposed by the prime minister, General Wojciech Jaruzelski, in December 1981. Shortly after the shipyard strike, in September 1980, Pope John Paul published his encyclical *Laborem Exercens* (On Human Work) in support of Solidarity, and he met with Walesa in 1983 in highly publicized talks.

Due to relentless anti-Communist agitation within Poland and pressure from Western governments, elections took place in 1989, and a Solidarity-led coalition government was formed with Solidarity's Tadeusz Mazowiecki as Poland's first non-Communist prime minister since 1948. At the end of 1990, Walesa became the president of Poland. Similar peaceful movements in other Soviet satellites were inspired by Solidarity and came to be known collectively as the Revolutions of 1989. Erosion of the Soviet bloc culminated in the fall of the Berlin Wall in November 1989. The Soviet Union was dissolved in December 1991.

Solidarity was able to succeed, in part, because of its broad coalition of workers, farmers, intellectuals, and the Church. When the pope had visited in 1979, ordinary Polish citizens had realized their ability to unite and organize to accomplish a common task. Karol Wojtila's community building had paid off.

Shots Ring Out

May 13, 1981, was a normal Wednesday. It was after 5:00 in the early evening, and the pope was conducting his regular weekly general audience with an estimated 10,000 people present. At the moment he was circling St. Peter's Square for the second time in an open vehicle. Beside him in the car sat his personal secretary, Monsignor Stanislaw Dziwisz, who much later would be named Archbishop of Krakow by Pope Benedict. John Paul had just finished kissing a young child and had handed her back to her proud parents.

Although the police report said four shots were fired, Monsignor Dziwisz remembers it this way: A shot rang out, followed by the sound of hundreds of pigeons taking flight. A second shot followed. The pope slumped into the arms of Monsignor Dziwisz, who was stunned. Who would attack this gentle man?

"Where?" asked the monsignor. "In the stomach," replied the pope. "Are you in pain?" he continued. "Yes," came the reply.

The pope was less than one week shy of his sixty-first birthday. He had been shot in the abdomen, right elbow, and the second finger of his left hand. Two women were also wounded by the bullets, one critically. The pope was rushed by ambulance to the Agostino Gemelli University Polyclinic (Hospital). Monsignor Dziwisz was asked by the pope's personal physician to perform the last anointing. Having hemorrhaged badly, John Paul received six pints of blood, some of which was donated by the doctors present. He then underwent nearly five-and-a-half hours of surgery during which parts of his intestine were removed in three places. Following his release he experienced a serious infection and again had to be hospitalized. Then he had to undergo a second operation to reverse his colostomy. Only in mid-August was he released from the hospital for the last time.

The attempt occurred on the anniversary of the day in 1917 when three shepherd children claimed they saw an apparition of the Virgin Mary in Fatima, Portugal. While still in the hospital, John Paul asked to see the so-called third secret that had been revealed to the children. He then credited Our Lady of Fatima with saving his life.

The wood-be assassin was an escaped murderer and small-time crook by the name of Mehmet Ali Agca. The 23-year-old Agca, a Turkish citizen with links to a Turkish ultranationalist group called the Gray Wolves, had escaped from prison while awaiting trial for the 1979 murder of a Turkish left-wing newspaper editor. He was convicted *in absentia*. He wrote a letter to a Turkish newspaper at the time and said he had escaped prison so that he could kill the pope, who was scheduled to visit Turkey. Two years later, when he was apprehended in St. Peter's Square, he had in his pocket several notes in Turkish, including one that read: "I am killing the Pope as a protest against the imperialism of the Soviet Union and the United

States and against the genocide that is being carried out in El Salvador and Afghanistan."

The pope publicly forgave Agca, but when he went to the prison to meet with Agca, he was troubled by the man's lack of remorse. Agca for his part wanted to know why the pope was still alive when he had fired off several good shots. Agca, too, blamed the Virgin of Fatima.

On May 13, 2000, at Fatima, the Vatican secretary of state revealed the third secret to an audience of 600,000 believers. He explained that the secret had not been revealed earlier so as not to promote speculation surrounding the cloaked information. The commentator on the secret was Cardinal Joseph Ratzinger, who at the time was head of the Vatican's Congregation for the Doctrine of the Faith but later became Pope Benedict. The written text of the secret described "a bishop dressed in white," whom the Portuguese children believed was the pope. This pope, "half trembling with halting step, afflicted with pain and sorrow," comes to the foot of a cross and is "killed by a group of soldiers who fired bullets and arrows at him." Then-Cardinal Ratzinger explained that the larger meaning of the message could be understood as the suffering state of the Church in the twentieth century and that Agca was not a tool of divine destiny. His fate had not been predetermined; rather, he had acted entirely with free will.

Although he never saw any proof to confirm the suspicion, John Paul believed the K.G.B. was behind the assassination attempt. Who else stood to gain by his death? With support for Solidarity swelling in Poland, he knew that the Soviet Union viewed him as a dangerous threat to the survival of communism. They were right, but whether they were involved in the attempt has never been determined.

Although sentenced to life in prison, Agca was pardoned by the Italian President Carlo Ciampi in June 2000 after serving nineteen years for the crime. He was then extradited to Turkey to complete his prison sentence for the murder of the Turkish journalist, and also for several robberies. He was freed from a Turkish prison in January 2010 at the age of 52.

Agca's mental state is thoroughly dubious. Although he had initially indicated Palestinian ties and K.G.B. and Bulgarian involvement in the attempt on the pope's life, he later disavowed those remarks. While anticipating his release from prison, he bizarrely applied to both Poland and Portugal (where Fatima is located) for citizenship but was denied it. After his release, he declared himself "Christ eternal." He further stated: "I proclaim the end of the world. All the world will be destroyed in this century. Every human being will die in this century." It has never been clear whether Agca is a madman or simply obfuscating.

As traumatic as the event was at the time, the pope recovered well and continued with his mission.

Mother Teresa

In February 1986, John Paul visited Mother Teresa's Nirmal Hriday Home for the Dying in Calcutta. There he tended to the afflicted. When he left, the pope hugged Mother Teresa. His experience with the afflicted had moved and upset him, and he was clearly grateful to Mother Teresa for her mission.

The two had first met in the early 1970s, but they developed a close friendship after John Paul's election as pope. She visited the pope whenever she was in Rome and apprised him of her work. He was naturally especially interested in her inroads into Communist countries. Because she was outspoken in her defense of the unborn, the pope asked her to spread this message for him because she could go to places he could not. Since her values so closely aligned with his, he felt he could trust her.

Mother Teresa had once joked that all her sisters should hasten to die because this pope (John Paul) was canonizing everyone. The reason behind John Paul's vigorous canonizing activity was this: because he believed that the road to sainthood was open to everyone, he wanted people in every nation to have their own saints to honor and hold as role models.

Upon hearing of Mother's Teresa's death, the pope expressed the wish that her sainthood would follow quickly. He was utterly convinced of her merits. As it happened, he opened and fast-tracked the cause for Mother Teresa's canonization less than two years later, waiving the usual five-year waiting period. She was beatified in 2003. On that occasion, John Paul called her "an icon of the Good Samaritan," who chose "to be not just *the least* but to be *the servant of the least.*"

A Leader for Youth

As is well-known, young people were a particular focus John Paul's pastoral care. He was concerned about them as the future of the Church. He was concerned about them as part of his vision for the family. He was concerned about them because of his emphasis on human dignity at all stages of life. And he was concerned about them for themselves.

From the beginning of his priesthood as a university chaplain, John Paul cared about the lives of young people. As early as the month following his election, the new pope was out meeting the young, in the first instance, addressing thousands of teenagers in Rome. He told them to spread the word about how much he relied upon them.

Due to his willingness to participate in honest dialogue with the youth of the world, he was able to engage them to an unprecedented degree. They loved his gentle banter, loving ways, and obvious concern. He even sang with them. They were simply mesmerized. In May 1980, he met for three hours with thousands of young people in the Parc des Princes stadium in Paris. The success of this event led to a series of World Youth Days. The 1993 World Youth Day in Denver drew 700,000 attendees despite predictions that secular young people simply weren't interested. At the University of Rome Tor Vergata in 2000, he drew a crowd of two million.

John Paul II and Gender Issues

Another group John Paul sought to engage was women. He has been accused of having had little understanding of women due to lifelong isolation from them. He did, after all, lose his mother at a young age and had no sisters or in-laws. This characterization hardly seems balanced, however. Karol Wojtila was not psychologically stunted. He was very active socially as a youth. He had female friends with whom he shared the stage. Women participated in the literary and academic circles in which he was involved. He knew many women quite well through his university chaplaincy and through his Catholic social and study circles. He had, in fact, interacted with women a great deal in his life.

If John Paul chose *not* to implement every change some women would have wanted, it wasn't because he didn't understand modern women and their aspirations. In many respects, he did understand modern women—the modern women of his youth in Poland. What he couldn't understand was why the Catholic feminists contemporary with his pontificate didn't agree with him.

John Paul was not a latecomer to the idea of women's advancement and representation. While still a professor at the Catholic University, he had attempted to have a nun, Sister Zofia Zdybicka, appointed to the faculty. As it happened, Sister Zofia's Ursuline superior denied her the opportunity, but permission was later granted by a different superior. He was also one of the few speakers to take notice of the female religious who were present at the Second Vatican Council, addressing them in his opening remarks.

John Paul was in many ways deeply sympathetic to the circumstances of women. He wrote movingly about women who struggled to earn a living, mothers whose adult children neglected them, and widows who lived with loneliness ("Apostolic Letter*Mulieris Dignitatem*of the Supreme PontiffJohn Paul IIon the*Dignity and Vocationof Womenon the Occasionof the Marian Year*," August 15, 1988).

His teachings on women accorded with his overarching commitment to the principle of human dignity. As pope, John Paul outspokenly defended women's basic humanity, a humanity he viewed as being complementary to the male but no less worthy. Complementarity was central to his view of the respective roles of men and women. Nevertheless, since man and woman were created equally human in the image of God, as taught in the Book of Genesis, both were entitled to fundamental dignity. (This had also been expressed in *Gaudium et Spes*.) Women's value is intrinsic, irrespective of her cultural setting, job, education, marital status, or personal attributes.

John Paul readily acknowledged the historic subjugation of women and affirmed the need to overturn it. Accordingly, his interpretation of Ephesians 5:22, "Wives, be subject to your husbands as to the Lord," involved husbands and wives being mutually subjugated to

80

each other in a relationship of reciprocal self-giving (*General Audience*, August 11, 1982).

He was unequivocal about the importance of women in the modern workforce, and he truly believed that allowing women to reach their potential would lead to the betterment of humanity. He even apologized for the role any members of the Church had played in the suppression of women and pointed to the need to follow Jesus' example in according women respect.

Within the Church, he tried to allow women a larger voice. During his pontificate, women participated as experts in synods and conferences. More women received placements in the departments of the Roman Curia, the administrative structure of the Holy See. In Latin America, where a shortage of priests was a chronic problem, he allowed an increase in the number of women serving as parish administrators. Women religious were permitted to conduct baptisms, burials, and prayer services, and to distribute previously consecrated hosts. And in 2004, for the first time, two women theologians were appointed to the International Theological Commission, and a woman was named to be president of the Pontifical Academy of Social Sciences.

All this accords well with the first stages of modern feminism. But there was a point beyond which John Paul was not prepared to go. He viewed certain contemporary behaviors as being culturally conditioned and running counter to the eternal teachings of the Church and the divine plan. He simply could not see alternative theological explanations or approaches to his positions on male priesthood, birth control, abortion, or gender identity. Toward the end of his life, he could be quite harsh in his opposition. He extolled women who were prepared to die in childbirth rather than undergo lifesaving abortions, or who suffered in abusive situations to preserve the sacrament of marriage. In one particularly insensitive moment, he went as far as to blame women for the bad behavior of men. He naively thought that reliance on moral education would cure all ills. And thus, he alienated large segments of Church membership with his views.

As far as the priesthood is concerned, John Paul held fast to the gender diversity of certain religious roles and the need for an exclusively male, celibate priesthood. He viewed the male priesthood as based in Christ's selection of male Apostles, a definitive tradition faithfully confirmed without deviation by both Catholic and Eastern Churches: a priest, as bridegroom of the Church, is a vital icon of Christ, the way God chose to become manifest on earth. This is not a matter of culturally conditioned discrimination against women but of preserving sacramental symbolism and efficacy.

As such, there was no room for change or debate, in John Paul's view. Instead, John Paul looked always to Mary, the first disciple, as the epitome of womanhood. Accordingly, he believed that virginity, not priesthood, was a proper course for women who sought to make gifts of themselves for God. He did not mean this in any way to diminish women's role and observed that the Church hierarchy only exists for the holiness of the faithful. Saints, not priests, he declared, are the most exalted among the faithful (*Ordinatio Sacerdotalis*, 1994). And he did his part to advance the causes of many women for exaltation within the Church.

Even so, his intransigence on divisive gender issues irked and frustrated many Catholics in the West, who bemoaned the pope's unyielding traditionalism. Whose position, they asked, is really the product of cultural conditioning?

A Dark Time

It must be said, first of all, that John Paul's strange reluctance to deal head-on with the crisis of sex abuse among the clergy continues to be mystifying, especially in light of his overall human rights record. In fact, the Vatican as a whole seems to have awakened to the fray only when forced to do so. There was extreme reluctance to confront the fact that a large number of supposedly righteous individuals were something other than what they professed. There may have been a tendency to view the accusations as overblown attempts to discredit the Church. Complicating matters further, some of the accused possessed a good deal—in some cases a great deal—of power and influence within the Church. Moreover, the hierarchical structures within the Curia that have sometimes supported misdeeds are even now still being investigated, as Pope Francis recently indicated. Here, then, is a very general summary of the situation under Pope John Paul II.

As an administrator, John Paul had always been known as a leader uninterested in details. He preferred to lay the course and then let the bureaucracy tend to itself. This allowed him to focus on his own programs and agenda.

As archbishop, he had made friends out of potential opponents and avoided schism by retaining in their posts clerics who did not see things or do things as he did. To avoid embarrassing specific individuals, even ineffectual people were retained in their positions until they could eventually be replaced, sometimes only upon death or retirement.

This is not to say that John Paul didn't listen to his "underlings." Certainly he took the bold step of giving the College of Cardinals a voice and role beyond that of electing popes every so often. Nevertheless, this management style may have contributed to the debacle in confronting the Church's child sex abuse scandals.

Alarms were already being raised in the United States during the 1950s, long before the pontificate of John Paul. Father Gerald Fitzgerald, founder of the Servants of the Paraclete, had tried to treat molesting priests and was convinced they could not be helped. He felt there needed to be a "uniform code of discipline and of penalties" for dealing with the priest. He communicated this position repeatedly to several U.S. bishops and to Vatican officials. In one 1952 letter to the Bishop of Reno, he stated that such priests should be laicized because the damage to Church should take precedence over concern for the individual priest. Real conversion on the part of offending priests was rare, he advised, and they posed a real danger if moved from diocese to diocese. In 1957 he received a letter from a New Hampshire bishop telling him about a repentant priest who needed a "fresh start." Fitzgerald responded that such priests only pretended to repent so that they could again be in a position to abuse. In many of the letters, Fitzgerald poured out his own disgust towards these priests, calling them "devils," "damned," and a "class of rattlesnake." He wanted—literally—to isolate them on an island, away from society. The letters were unsealed by a court in 2007 and made public by the *National Catholic Reporter* in a series of articles in 2009.

In another major instance, credible allegations about the sexual abuse of children by a particular priest were made during the pontificate of Paul VI and thereafter. Two Mexican priests working in the United States accused the influential founder of the Legion of Christ, Father Marcial Maciel Degollado, of abusing them repeatedly while they were children. Over time, there were reports of dozens who had been abused by just that one priest. Although the local U.S. bishop made a full report to the Vatican representative in Washington, D.C., the report seems to have been shelved at the curial level. A letter addressed to Pope John Paul by one of the victim priests also contained some of the information about that particular case, but it is not known whether John Paul ever saw the letter personally. Other letters from other victims followed and were ignored.

It is not clear at precisely what point John Paul became aware, or was made aware, of increasing numbers of allegations about criminal priestly behavior. Certainly, the crisis extended far beyond being a mere "detail," and warranted his full attention. There is every indication that through the 1980s John Paul knew or should have known—the U.S. Bishops were virtually pleading for help—but failed to act. Some officials within the Vatican itself complained that their leaders failed to grasp the gravity of the problem, whereas others couldn't understand why the U.S. bishops were speaking so openly about it all. The March 2000 Day of Penance Mass mentioned "minors who are victims of abuse," among others mistreated but was not terribly specific.

John Paul finally took decisive action in April 2002 by calling in his American bishops to discuss the matter. Consistent with his managerial style, he left it to them to resolve the problem, but he also made it clear that they needed to address it. It's possible that in taking this course of action, he meant to bypass any obstructions in the Curia, but it was also evident that systemic changes in the Church in the United States needed to be made. This is not to say that the problem of abuse existed only in the United States; however, the major effort was made not within the Church as a whole, but rather where the wheel was squeakiest.

(Other parts of the world are more reticent about holding public debate on such issues. Along with the United States, the English-speaking countries of Australia, Canada, and Great Britain were also more vocal than other parts of the world about the problem.)

In his address to the U.S. cardinals, John Paul stated that he was "deeply grieved" that people who were supposed to be living holy lives had caused such suffering to young people. He continued by stating that abuse by clerics was "by every standard wrong and rightly considered a crime by society; it is also an appalling sin in the eyes of God." He included this message to those most directly affected: "To the victims and their families, wherever they may be, I express my profound sense of solidarity and concern." He stated in no uncertain terms that there was "no place in the priesthood and religious life for those who would harm the young," and he reaffirmed the Church's commitment to sexual morality and the good of married and family life. Nevertheless, he also expressed a view that may historically have been behind some of the hierarchical foot-dragging; namely, that even the perpetrators could be changed by Christian conversion (Address to the Cardinals of the United States and Conference Officers, April 23, 2002). When similar scandals broke in the Philippines in 2003-04, the pope spoke about the need for Christian mercy in dealing with the priests involved, although he did also talk about transparency and "strict discipline" for the common good.

Following the meetings between the pope and the U.S. bishops, spokespersons for the United States Conference of Catholic Bishops expressed disappointment that the media was focusing its attention exclusively on old cases of abuse and had not taken notice of any new measures that had been put in place over the prior ten to fifteen years to prevent such abuses from occurring. Discussing instances when pedophile priests had been reassigned to similar duties in other parishes where they were free to abuse again, they pointed out that those priests had been treated with psychotherapy, and it was thought at the time that this was sufficient. Now, the reality of recidivism was better understood, and bishops were not likely to make the same mistake. Bishop Wilton Gregory, then-president of the Conference, stated that any pedophile priests in the future would have to be turned over to civil authorities and should always have been. He further stated that the pope had a "high level of understanding" of the situation and had personally expressed to him his concern for the spirit of the people, the priests, and the bishops of the United States.

The U.S. Conference of Bishops met in June 2002 and in response to the crisis adopted a comprehensive set of national standards and procedures, the *Charter for the Protection of Children and Young People*. The *Charter's* adoption followed meetings with victims and their families and with experts on sexual abuse and its impact on survivors, and it took into account the opinions of the Catholic laity. It was approved with revisions at the June 2011 General Meeting of the U.S. Catholic Bishops. In addition, *Essential Norms for Diocesan/Eparchial Policies Dealing with Allegations of Sexual Abuse of Minors by Priests or Deacons* was recognized by the Vatican and promulgated in 2006.

The "Preamble" to the *Charter* acknowledges the breach of trust involved in past failures. The *Charter* commits the dioceses to working with victims for healing and reconciliation through social services and counseling, and to involve laity to a greater degree in the pertinent processes. It expresses a zero tolerance for abuse and abusers, stating that if a priest is found to be an abuser in even one instance "the offending priest or deacon is to be permanently removed from ministry and, if warranted, dismissed from the clerical state." It also made provisions for transparency and accountability.

Victims, their families and supporters, and dismayed Church members wanted to hear Pope John Paul speak to them directly and unambiguously, but he failed to do so. The problem still has not been thoroughly addressed on a global scale. Many in the United States would consider John Paul's handling of the crisis to be the single biggest failure of his pontificate.

The most recent statements by the Church on the subject of clerical abuse of minors, including the instructions to bishops dating to 1962 (*Crimen Sollicitationis*), can be found at the Vatican website: http://www.vatican.va/resources/index_en.htm.

Interreligious Dialogue

John Paul was a student of culture, and he had deep respect for the diversity of world culture, including its religious components. He repeatedly taught that the diversity of peoples must be respected for peace to progress. He was firmly committed to religious freedom for all people and to freedom from coercion of conscience. Freedom from coercion meant that the forceful conversions of the past were unacceptable. Based on Vatican II and his own belief in the shared dignity of human beings as creatures of a universal God, the pope continually promoted interreligious dialogue and respect for non-Christian religions.

Following the teachings of Vatican II, he believed there are elements in all religions that advance the good in humans and in society. Addressing Portuguese Christian, Jewish, and Muslim leaders in 1982, he affirmed "the undeniable treasures of every religion's spirituality." The March 2000 Day of Pardon Mass included a confession of "enmity towards members of other religions" and prayed for repentance among Christians.

Pope John Paul was convinced that prayer could bring together the believers of diverse faiths, an idea that inspired the 1986 World Day of Prayer for Peace in Assisi, Italy. That unprecedented gathering drew together 160 religious leaders representing many distinct groups, including Jews, Buddhists, Shintoists, Muslims, Zoroastrians, Hindus, Unitarians, and traditional African and Native

American religions, in addition to many Christians of different denominations. Together, they prayed for world peace.

Still, he observed, part of truth is recognizing where differences exist, while respecting the boundaries that divide us.

Christian Ecumenism

John Paul wholeheartedly sought reunification of the Christian world. The second millennium of Christianity had been a period of schism in the Church, and with the third millennium of Christianity approaching, he felt the time was right for reconciliation. He especially hoped for rapprochement with the Orthodox Church.

In his 1995 Encyclical *Ut Unum Sint* (That They May Be One), the pope urged putting aside prejudices so that with prayer and "mutual forgiveness and reconciliation," it might be possible to examine and overcome the divisions of the past. His eye was on nothing less than "full communion among Christ's disciples." Nevertheless, "In matters of faith, compromise is in contradiction with God who is Truth.... who could consider legitimate a reconciliation brought about at the expense of the truth?" There was obviously only so far he could—or would—go. Still, as a student of culture, he knew well that truth could be expressed in different forms. He encouraged joint prayer among Christians, even when not in full communion, as a way of bringing about Christian unity.

The Anglican Communion

The Anglican Communion today consists of approximately 85 million people in 165 countries. While Anglican/Episcopalian churches maintain full communion, each national or regional church is autonomous.

In 1980 John Paul II issued the so-called Pastoral Provision, which allowed former Episcopal priests to enter into full communion with the Catholic Church and to become Catholic priests. It made possible the ordination of married priests under those limited circumstances. It also allowed the acceptance of former Episcopal parishes into the Catholic Church and allowed the retention of certain Anglican liturgical elements within those parishes. According to the Pastoral Provision website (http://www.pastoralprovision.org/), from 1983 to the present more than one hundred men have been ordained as priests and three such parishes were established under the Pastoral Provision. (In 2012, Pope Benedict XVI established the Personal Ordinariate of the Chair of St. Peter for groups of Anglicans in the United States seeking to enter into full communion with the Catholic Church. The Pastoral Provision remains the path for priestly ordination, however.)

In 1982, John Paul became the first reigning pope to visit the United Kingdom, where he preached in Canterbury Cathedral and met with the Archbishop of Canterbury and Queen Elizabeth, who is the Supreme Governor of the Church of England, with the authority to appoint bishops, archbishops, and deans of cathedrals. He was ultimately disappointed by the Church of England's decision to admit women to the priesthood, which he saw as an obstacle to unity. In 2003, he spoke obliquely about the appointment of a gay Episcopal bishop in the U.S. and the blessing of same-gender marriages in Canada, telling the Archbishop of Canterbury that it was necessary to protect the faith from "misguided interpretations." On the positive side, joint commissions were able to reach agreement on several doctrinal points, and the pope expressed commitment to pursuing the course despite difficulties.

John Paul II and Eastern Orthodoxy

Today, there are an estimated 225–300 million members of Eastern Orthodox Churches. Important steps toward reconciliation with the Orthodox Churches had already taken place under John XXIII and Paul VI. John Paul viewed the Eastern Churches and the Western Church as the two lungs of a single entity. He believed that with faith, prayer, study, and goodwill, the answers to difficult issues would emerge. He wanted to establish full communion between the two, or as he later put it, "full unity in legitimate diversity" (*Ut Unum Sint,* "On Commitment to Ecumenism," 1995). As in the case of gender-specific roles, he described legitimate differences among the Western and various Eastern Churches as cases of "complementarity."

Consequently, his own follow-up to the earlier papal efforts was almost immediate. In November 1979, he visited the Ecumenical Patriarch Dimitrios I of the See of Constantinople and laid the groundwork for future theological discussions. A *Joint International Commission for the Theological Dialogue between the Catholic Church and the Orthodox Church* was established to work towards full communion, the goal of which was common celebration of the Eucharist.

Patriarch Dimitrios paid a return visit to Rome, but not until 1987. This delay would seem to indicate that the patriarch did not place as high a premium on reunification as the pope. Apparent foot-dragging notwithstanding, delegations from both Sees routinely visited each other for their respective celebrations.

One outcome of those discussions was recognition of the Eastern Catholic Church's right to its own organization and apostolate. This was meant to smooth relations between Eastern Catholics (already in full communion with the Catholic Church) and Orthodox living in the same territories. The pope claimed a lessening of tensions as a result.

John Paul was able to further relations with a number of other leaders of Eastern Churches, including Pope Shenouda III of the Coptic Orthodox Church; the Syrian Patriarch of Antioch, Mor Ignatius Zakka I; and the Venerable Patriarch of the Ethiopian Church, Abuna Paulos. He was also able to sign a common Christological declaration with the Assyrian Patriarch of the East, Mar Dinkha IV.

In May 1999, he visited Romania on the invitation of Patriarch Teoctist Arapasu of the Romanian Orthodox Church, the first time a pope had visited a predominantly Eastern Orthodox country since the so-called Great Schism in 1054. He followed this up with a visit in June 2001 to the Ukraine, where he spoke to leaders of the All-Ukrainian Council of Churches and Religious Organizations.

To his disappointment, the Russian Orthodox Church continued to be resistant to Vatican overtures, and he was never able to visit either Russia or Belorus. At the Church of the Holy Sepulcher, where each Church has staked out its inch of turf and hostilities are open and raw, the aged Greek Patriarch of Jerusalem, Diodorus, personally kept the pope from using the main entrance.

Nevertheless, John Paul was willing to endure personal humiliation for the sake of his goal. In 2001, he visited Greece, becoming the first pope to visit in nearly 1300 years. Archbishop Christodoulos, the leader of the Greek Orthodox Church, had been pressured by his government into receiving the pope, and he wasn't happy about it. The Archbishop observed that many of his faithful were opposed to the pope being there, and he presented John Paul with a list of "thirteen offences" made by the Catholic Church against the Orthodox Church since the Great Schism, including the horrible sack of Christian Constantinople by the Crusaders in 1204. The Archbishop then pointed out that no apology had ever been made for any of these offences. John Paul then asked for pardon. The delighted Archbishop clapped his hands. (Actually, he had been told before the trip that the pope planned to apologize.) Thereafter, the two issued a joint statement that included a condemnation of violence in the name of religion, and they prayed the Lord's Prayer together in private, breaking an Orthodox prohibition on praying with Catholics.

Meeting with such far-flung figures gave the pope a joy somewhat analogous to the biblical ingathering of the exiles.

John Paul II and Buddhism

In 1984, the pope conducted Mass in Bangkok, Thailand, where he praised "the fruits of the 'peaceable' and 'gentle' wisdom" of Thai Buddhism and the "spiritual quality" of the Thai people. Similarly, during a visit to Sri Lanka in 1995, the pope spoke of his high regard for Buddhists and the virtues of Buddhism, and he affirmed his desire for interreligious dialogue and cooperation.

John Paul he met with the fourteenth Dalai Lama eight times. Since both religious leaders came from Communist-repressed societies, it was to be expected they would have much to discuss. Nevertheless, the Vatican tended to downplay such meetings because of its desire to improve relations with China, a fact the Dalai Lama understood and acknowledged. While most Catholics considered these meetings emblematic of the pope's expansive heart, rejectionist Catholics who deny Vatican II saw it simply as more cavorting by the "anti-pope" with pagans and idolaters.

Even so, in his 1994 book, *Crossing the Threshold of Hope,* he counseled the faithful against incorporating seemingly innocuous Buddhist elements into their personal practices, and he emphasized the differences between Catholicism and Buddhism. As described by John Paul, Christianity and Buddhism are opposing systems of belief. Both revolve around soteriology, but the salvation expressed in Buddhism is a "negative soteriology" seeking detachment from an evil world that causes only sorrow. In addition, the detachment achieved in Buddhism does not have the goal of bringing one closer to God. Thus, Buddhism's focus is quite different and incompatible with Catholicism. He described Buddhism as being "in large measure an 'atheistic' system," a characterization which some Buddhists found offensive. To soothe those offended, the pope later emphasized again his respect for Buddhism.

John Paul II and Islam

Many Muslims appreciated the overtures John Paul made to improve Catholic–Muslim dialogue. He was the first pope to visit an officially Islamic country at the invitation of its religious leader. This occurred in August 1985, when he visited Morocco at the behest of King Hassan II. During that visit, he enjoyed a visit with thousands of Muslim young people in Casablanca Stadium, emphasizing: "we believe in the same God, the one God, the living God." In May 2001 he became the first pope in history to enter a mosque, the Umayyad Mosque in Damascus, Syria, which had formerly been a Byzantine church. At the mosque, he said that Christians and Muslims had often offended one another and needed to offer each other forgiveness, a theme he repeated elsewhere as well.

In 1974, Pope Paul VI had created the Commission for Religious Relations with Muslims as a section within the Pontifical Council for non-Christians, which he had also established. In 1998, during the pontificate of John Paul, a Joint Committee was established between the Pontifical Council for Interreligious Dialogue and the Permanent Committee of al-Ahzar for Dialogue with Monotheistic Religions. The Islamic University of al-Azhar in Cairo is the highest religious institution in Egypt. The joint committee met at least once a year for a number of years, alternating between Cairo and in Rome. In 2000, the pope had a cordial meeting in Egypt with Sheikh Mohammed Sayyed Tantawi, the well-respected Grand Imam of al-Azhar whose later denunciations of violence against Christians in Egypt were much appreciated by Christians. (Sheikh Tantawi died in 2010, and relations with the Vatican were suspended by his successor. Many other initiatives with the Muslim world, however, took place both before and after that date.) The annual papal message for World Peace Day, established by Pope Paul VI in 1968, continued to be regularly translated into Arabic, and John Paul continued the tradition begun by Paul VI of addressing an annual message of goodwill to all Muslims for the end of the Islamic holy month of Ramadan.

John Paul's views concerning Islam were rooted in the statement on Islam in *Nostra Aetate*, which credits Islam with belief in the one God, valuing prayer, and esteeming morality. On numerous occasions, John Paul emphasized the commonality of Christianity, Islam, and Judaism as spiritual descendants of Abraham sharing worship of the one God who created the world. He viewed that common witness as a key point of cohesion among the three monotheistic religions against an increasingly secular world. He particularly admired the Islamic fidelity to prayer since prayer was so central to his own life and spirituality, and he called it a model for Christians. He expressed the hope that dialogue would lead to improved knowledge and esteem between the two religions, but he also emphasized the need to renounce violence as a means for resolving any differences.

John Paul preached respect for the rights of Muslims to practice their faith, but he lamented that Christians did not have this right in countries like Saudi Arabia, where even the possession of a Bible is a crime. He was deeply concerned about the persecution of Christians in parts of Africa and Asia under Islamic religious law or influence, and he called for mutual respect and religious freedom in predominantly Muslim countries.

John Paul II and the Jewish People

The effort to improve and maintain Catholic–Jewish relations was a hallmark of John Paul's pontificate. The realization of the loss of Poland's Jewish community, including people who had been close to him, seemed to haunt John Paul.

The pope once referred to the Jews of Poland as having "lived arm in arm with us for generations" (*Jasna Gora Meditation*, September 26, 1990). Indeed, this was true. The Jews in Poland dated back to at least as early as the 10th century. Prior to World War II, Poland held the largest Jewish community in Europe, with 3.3 million Jews. Only 11% survived the war, approximately 369,000 people. A number of those who survived either did not return to Poland or managed to flee as refugees. By 1948, only 100,000 Jews remained in Poland. These, like the Catholics of Poland, had to cope with an anti-religious Communist regime.

During the Stalinist years, Jewish culture and religion were brutally suppressed. After Stalin's death in 1953, there was the beginning of a Jewish cultural revival, and in the years 1958-59, Jews were permitted to emigrate to Israel but nowhere else. Fifty thousand availed themselves of the opportunity. The 1967 Six-Day War in Israel brought another round of suppression in Poland. Today, there are estimated to be only 5,000 to 10,000 Jews in Poland.

As a priest in Poland, Father Wojtila had counseled young Poles to visit and care for the abandoned Jewish cemeteries of Krakow, using it as an opportunity to educate them about the historic presence of the Jews now largely missing from Polish society. As Archbishop of Krakow, he maintained close relations with the surviving Jewish community of Krakow. As pope, however, John Paul was able to paint on a broader canvas.

While Archbishop Wojtila was in Rome participating in the Second Vatican Council, he was able to renew his friendship with his old friend Jerzy Kluger, who he found had survived the war after all, having joined the Polish army in exile. Jerzy had participated in the liberation of Italy from the Nazis and by coincidence was now living in Rome. (His grandmother, mother, and sister—well-known to young Karol Wojtila—had all been killed in the death camps. His father had also survived as an officer in the Polish army, ironically stationed in British-mandate Palestine.) It may be that becoming reacquainted with Jerzy drew interreligious issues back to the forefront of the pontiff's thoughts, but they had never altogether left the concerns of this deep-thinking and compassionate man.

John Paul became the first pope to visit a Nazi death camp (Auschwitz in 1979), although he had done so earlier, in 1973, as a cardinal. He was the first pope since Saint Peter to visit a synagogue, the Great Synagogue of Rome, which occurred in 1986. In his speech at the Great Synagogue, he affirmed that Christianity had a uniquely close relationship with Judaism, calling Jews "dearly beloved brothers" and "elder brothers" (the latter reference citing the great Polish poet Adam Mickiewicz, a favorite of the pope's). In addition, he cited "the Dogmatic Constitution *Lumen Gentium,* no. 16, referring to Saint Paul in the Letter to the Romans (11:28-29), that the Jews are beloved of God, who has called them with an irrevocable calling."

In 1987, the pope met with the Jewish leadership of Poland, where he called Jewish witness to the Holocaust (using the Hebrew term "Shoah") a prophetic "warning voice for all humanity." That same year, while in the United States, he called for Holocaust education to be integrated into every level of Catholic education. He further called for world recognition of the Jewish right "to a homeland." In 1990, when meeting with the ambassador of the newly reunited Germany, he remarked: "For Christians the heavy burden of guilt for the murder of the Jewish people must be an enduring call to repentance."

The reemergence of Israel as a state had for some time been doctrinally awkward for the Vatican, but in December 1993, the Vatican and Israel reached a *Fundamental Agreement Between the Holy See and the State of Israel,* and in 1994 finally exchanged ambassadors and normalized relations.

In his Apostolic Letter *Tertio Millennio Adveniente* (November 1994), John Paul had asked Catholics to prepare for the new millennium by examining occasions of Christian sinfulness. In response to that call, in 1998, the Vatican's Commission for Religious Relations with the Jews promulgated a major document of self-examination, *We Remember: A Reflection on the Shoah*, with an introduction by John Paul. Calling the Holocaust "a major fact of the history of this century," it takes responsibility for the relationship between Nazism and the attitudes of Christians toward Jews down through the centuries. Accordingly, the importance of this document for Catholic self-evaluation cannot be overstated.

We Remember was followed in March 2000 by a Day of Pardon Mass, which included confession of sins against Israel. Later that month, the pope made a five-day pilgrimage to the State of Israel, where he visited Yad Vashem and also placed a prayer in the Western Wall in accordance with Jewish custom. The friendly style of that visit (the Israeli code name for the security operations during the visit was actually "Operation Old Friend") was in marked contrast to the 11-hour visit by Paul VI in 1964, during which he never mentioned Israel by name and refused to address the Israeli president (Zalman Shazar) by his title.

There were numerous other occasions when John Paul met with representatives of Jewish communities in various parts of the world and spoke words of reconciliation.

Not everything the pope did found favor in the Jewish community. John Paul acknowledged that there would be times when Jewish and

Catholic interests would not coincide. During his papacy, conflict revolved around three main issues: a group of Carmelite nuns who had located their convent at Auschwitz, audiences granted to people anathema to the Jewish community, and the candidacy for sainthood of Catholics who had been hostile to Jews in their lifetimes.

The controversy of longest duration involved the Auschwitz convent. There was a strong tendency in Poland to "de-judaize" the site, where approximately 1.3 million Jews died. The Polish government subsumed all peoples within the common classification of victims of fascism and failed to make any mention of Jews as particular targets for genocide. Tour guides of Auschwitz did not mention Jews, nor did the official guidebook to the museum. Then, in 1984, a group of Polish Catholic nuns moved into a two-story building that had been used by the Nazis to store the deadly Zyklon B gas used in the gas chambers. Sensitivities on both sides were inflamed. Finally, in 1993, on the fiftieth anniversary of the (Jewish) Warsaw ghetto uprising, the pope personally sent a letter to the Carmelite nuns telling them to move to a new property a short distance away which had been built for them and to which they had thus far refused to move. They complied.

The timing of two papal audiences was particularly unfortunate. Not all Christians were thrilled either when in 1982 PLO Chairman Yassir Arafat met with the pope. At the time it was assumed that it was Arafat's minions who were responsible for the assassination only days before of Bachir Gemayel, the Christian president-elect of Lebanon. The assassination further inflamed the interreligious civil war in Lebanon, resulting in the slaughter by the Christian Phalangist militia of Palestinians in Beirut's Sabra and Shatila refugee camps.

Pope John Paul met with Arafat a total of twelve times during his pontificate. Over that time the pope was disappointed about the lack of progress in peace talks. In his meetings, the pope stressed to Arafat that a solution "excluded recourse to violence in any form." One reason for the meetings was the pope's concern for the approximately 40,000 Christians who resided in the disputed territories and would require religious protections under any future Palestinian government.

The second controversial audience was in 1987 with Kurt Waldheim, former secretary general of the United Nations and recently elected president of Austria. Waldheim's long concealed past as a Nazi officer had recently come to light during the Austrian election. This would be Waldheim's first official visit outside Austria since being elected president, a largely ceremonial role. Most of Europe responded to his election by making it clear he would not be welcome in their countries, while the United States Justice Department barred him from entry. Unlike Germany, Austria had done little to acknowledge, confront, and purge its Nazi past. It preferred to think of itself as having been forcibly occupied by the

Nazis and not complicit with them, despite all evidence to the contrary. Perhaps the pope had this in mind when on a trip to Austria in 1986 he had called anti-Semitism "sinful."

Waldheim had always asserted that he never belonged to any Nazi-affiliated groups, but in fact, only one month after the Anschluss (the German entry into Austria), at the age of nineteen, he joined the National Socialist German Students League, a Nazi youth organization. Then in November 1938, he enrolled in the SA, Nazi storm troopers. Waldheim further denied personal knowledge of wartime atrocities, yet he was a lieutenant in army intelligence attached to brutal German military units that executed thousands of (non-Jewish) Yugoslavian partisans and civilians and deported thousands of Greek Jews to death camps from 1942 to 1944. He served on the staff of Gen. Alexander Lohr, who was hanged for war crimes in 1947. Yet in his memoirs Waldheim wrote that he was a law student in Vienna at the time.

Waldheim's version of events was disproven by a mass of evidence: witnesses, photographs, medals, commendations, and his own signature on documents connected with massacres and deportations.

There was considerable speculation about why John Paul would receive Waldheim. Prior to becoming pope, he had been instrumental in post-war rapprochement between German and Polish Catholic bishops, and perhaps some gesture towards healing or redemption was involved in his meeting with Waldheim, but the pope failed to make his reasoning clear. The Vatican denied Waldheim had been invited, saying that audiences were always sought and that the pope never made invitations. They stressed that this was an official meeting, not a private one, and that Waldheim was returning a visit the Pope made to Austria in 1983. They further emphasized that the pope's meetings did not imply approval or disapproval because he was prepared to meet with people whose behavior he did not necessarily condone. Nevertheless, in a thoroughly puzzling move, John Paul followed up the audience several years later (1994) by awarding Waldheim a knighthood in the Order of Pius IX.

At the time of the audience, one American Jewish leader called Waldheim's visit "morally and politically incomprehensible." Others used harsher words. A number of Catholics were also bewildered. A demonstration took place outside the gates of the Vatican. One of the protestors was a Yugoslavian priest, Father Ivan Florianc, who said he was sure St. Peter would not have invited Waldheim. He added that he felt anger towards his spiritual leader for sitting down with dictators in Latin America and for receiving Waldheim.

The canonization of Father Maximilian Kolbe and the beatification of Pius IX were also disturbing to many Jews. Kolbe, who was especially revered by John Paul, was remembered by the Jewish community as having been far from a saint. While no one disputed

Father Kolbe's final selfless act of sacrificing his own life to save the life of another Pole in Auschwitz, he had been known before the war for publishing a damaging anti-Semitic Catholic newspaper.

Pope Pius IX, for his part, had been at the heart of an international scandal known as the Mortara Affair, which began in 1858. A six-year-old Jewish boy named Edgardo Mortara was secretly baptized by a Christian housekeeper (or at least, so she claimed). He was then essentially kidnapped from his parents by the papal police under orders of the Holy Office that were authorized by Pope Pius. The boy was reared by Pius and educated in Catholic seminaries. He was never returned to his parents, despite appeals from international governments, and became a priest. At the time, Pius complained that "the dogs" in Rome were making too much noise. Among those protesting Pius' elevation were descendants of the Mortara family.

Another source of irritation for Jews was the canonization of Sister Teresa Benedicta (Edith Stein), who had died at Auschwitz for being Jewish. She was not similarly reviled, but canonizing her smacked of co-opting (Catholicizing) the Jewish experience of the Holocaust, especially in light of the convent at Auschwitz. It should be remembered that Jews have long experienced this sense of misappropriation due to Christian interpretations of Hebrew Scriptures that accuse them of not understanding their own sacred texts. The pope, perhaps, saw it differently. In a way, it was as close as he could get as a Catholic to canonizing Jewish suffering. His remarks on the occasion of her canonization said: "From now on, as we celebrate the memory of this new saint from year to year, we must also remember the Shoah (Holocaust)…"

In sum, John Paul's own Polish background led him to feel a unique closeness to the Jewish people. He did everything he could to further amity between Jews and Catholics, without relinquishing the other points of his ecclesiastical agenda.

Infirmity and Death

The first sign of trouble came in 1991 with trembling in some fingers of the left hand. Then, in 1993, the pope fell and dislocated his right shoulder. His personal physician suspected a problem with balance and determined that the cause was Parkinson's disease, a brain malady that affects mainly the elderly and results in tremors, muscle spasms and rigidity, slowed movement, loss of balance, and other potentially severe symptoms. John Paul maintained a normal schedule for as long as he was able but then had to begin curtailing his activities. As was to be expected, he accepted the condition of his body as God's will, but he didn't like having to rely others for his mobility.

In January 2005, the pope was making his Angelus address but had difficulty speaking. The spasms became worse until by dinner it was difficult for him to breath. He was treated at the Agostino Gemelli University Polyclinic and recovered. The problem recurred, however, and on February 23, one of the cardinals eating dinner with the pope became so alarmed that he administered the sacrament of anointing. The next day the pope was brought back to Gemelli, where a tracheotomy was performed. On Easter Sunday, John Paul attempted to deliver his *Urbi et Orbi* ("to the City [of Rome] and to the World") benediction but had no voice left. He had to be content with making the sign of the cross and waving to the crowd of pilgrims in the square. On March 30 he again appeared at his window because he wanted to speak to a crowd of 5,000 young people who had come from Milan. Again his voice failed him.

Monsignor Dziwisz, who had now been Karol Wojtila's personal secretary for nearly forty years, had the impression that the pope at that point recognized his time was near and had accepted it.

The next day, March 31, the pope was in his private chapel celebrating Mass when he became extremely ill and experienced a very high fever. The doctors determined it was Septic shock caused by a urinary tract infection. John Paul's body was shutting down. In medical terms, he was experiencing cardiovascular collapse. It was now a matter of waiting. There would be no more extraordinary medical measures. John Paul had already made the decision not to return to the hospital. The goal now was to make him comfortable in his room during his final hours. He spent the time remaining to him in prayer and saying goodbye to those close to him.

John Paul had always maintained the habit of reading Scripture daily for spiritual renewal. Even on his final day, April 2, he asked to hear reading from the Gospel of John. Meanwhile, the crowd had swelled outside in Saint Peter's Square. They were shouting the pope's name and crying, "Viva il Papa." At one point, John Paul whispered to a nun attending him, "Let me go home to the Lord." Those were his last words. He fell into a coma that evening. Mass was performed in his room, and John Paul was given a few drops of wine as *viaticum*. The pope breathed his last at 9:37 that night. Those present in the room tearfully sang *Te Deum* in thanks to God for the life of the man who had just departed.

Much of the world mourned the passing of this gentle pope. Those who remembered the vigorous, young man he was when first elected, paused to reflect on their own mortality.

More than three million people flowed to Rome to honor John Paul.

Legacy

John Paul's pontificate lasted nearly twenty-seven years, one of the longest in papal history. During that time he had an unprecedented amount of contact with the public, including Catholics, non-Catholics, and foreign leaders. He made 104 pastoral visits outside Italy, and 146 within. The Vatican estimates that more than 17.6 million pilgrims participated in his regular Wednesday general audiences alone. He made 38 official visits and met with government leaders on 984 different occasions.

Because of his particular concern for the young, he established World Youth Days, nineteen of which were celebrated during his pontificate. He similarly initiated the World Meetings of Families in 1994. He called into being only the second Marian Year in history, and decreed a Year of the Redemption and Year of the Eucharist in order to promote spiritual renewal. He led the Church into the third millennium through his earlier voice in the Second Vatican Council and by proclaiming as pope a Holy Year Jubilee for the year 2000.

He organized numerous assemblies of the Synod of Bishops and the College of Cardinals, and created 231 Cardinals, substantially expanding the College of Cardinals and providing greater representation to all parts of the world. He gave the College of Cardinals a greater voice.

He met with leaders of other Christian Churches in an outreach of ecumenism. He improved relations with the Eastern Orthodox

Church and the Anglican Communion. He advanced dialogue with Judaism and Islam, as well as other religions.

To encourage spiritual growth among his followers, he held 147 beatification ceremonies for 1,338 individuals, and 51 canonization ceremonies naming 482 saints. His enthusiasm for saints was meant to encourage the faithful by providing role models for holiness and reasons for hope.

He issued many important teachings as pope and wrote five books as a private scholar.

He worked wholeheartedly for world peace.

At John Paul's funeral, the crowds clamored for his sainthood. "Santo subito," they yelled: "Sainthood now!" Pope Benedict XVI waived the normal five-year waiting period before beginning the cause of beatification and canonization for John Paul II. The cause was officially opened on June 28, 2005. A French nun, Sister Marie Simon-Pierre, was miraculously cured of Parkinson's disease after praying for John Paul's intercession. The rite for his beatification followed, fittingly enough, on May 1, 2011. May Day, while ironically a Communist holiday, is devoted in the Catholic calendar to the Blessed Virgin Mary, to whom John Paul was so devoted.

Word was released in June 2013 of a second miracle being approved by the Congregation for the Causes of Saints. The second miracle related to a Costa Rican woman, Floribeth Mora, whose cerebral aneurism was inexplicably cured on May 1, 2011, the day of John Paul's beatification.

On July 5, Pope Francis approved John Paul for sainthood, saying that Pope John XXIII and John Paul II will be canonized together. The date has not yet been established, although December 8, the Feast of the Immaculate Conception has been suggested. Irrespective of the details, John Paul's canonization appears imminent.

From Poland, John Paul's longtime private secretary, Cardinal Stanislaw Dziwisz, rejoiced at the news. "I thank God that I will live to see the elevation to sainthood the person who I served with love to the last beating of his heart," he stated. Abraham Foxman, as director of the Jewish organization the Anti-Defamation League, received four audiences with Pope John Paul. He spoke for John Paul's numerous supporters when he said, "For many of us Pope John Paul is already a saint, this just formalizes it."

The Pope and the Rosary

In 2002, before his death, Pope John Paul II wrote an Apostolic Letter entitled The Rosary of the Virgin Mary. He wrote about his love and daily practice of the rosary:

> The Rosary is my favorite prayer. A marvelous prayer! Marvelous in its simplicity and its depth...Against the background of the words Ave Maria the principal events of the life of Jesus Christ pass before the eyes of the soul. They take shape in the complete series of the joyful, sorrowful and glorious mysteries...

He urged all Catholics to recite the rosary:

> Dear brothers and sisters! A prayer so easy and yet so rich truly deserves to be rediscovered by the Christian community...I look to all of you of every state of life, to you, Christian families, to you, the sick and elderly, and to you, young people: confidently take up the Rosary once again. Rediscover the Rosary in the light of Scripture, in harmony with the liturgy, and in the conduct of your daily lives. May this appeal of mine not go unheard!

The rosary beads are an important component of the Catholic religion. Rosary beads are prayer beads used to count the series of prayers that make up the rosary.

The prayers consist of repeated sequences of the Lord's Prayer followed by ten prayings of the Hail Mary and a single praying of "Glory Be to the Father" and is sometimes accompanied by the Fatima Prayer. Each of these sequences is known as a decade. The praying of each decade is accompanied by meditation on one of the Mysteries of the Rosary, which recall the life of Jesus Christ.

The following is a brief overview of how to pray the rosary:

First, begin by holding the cross and repeating the "Sign of the Cross."

Sign of the Cross

In The Name of the Father and of the Son and of the Holy Spirit.

Then, "The Apostle's Creed" is said on the Cross.

The Apostle's Creed

I believe in God, the Father Almighty, Creator of heaven and earth and in Jesus Christ, His only Son, our Lord; Who was conceived by the Holy Spirit, born of the Virgin Mary, suffered under Pontius Pilate, was crucified, died, and was buried, He descended into hell; the third day He arose again from the dead; He ascended into Heaven, sitteth at the right hand of God, the Father Almighty, from thence He shall come to judge the living and the dead. I believe in the Holy Spirit, the Holy Catholic Church, the communion of saints, the forgiveness of sins, the resurrection of the body, and life everlasting. Amen.

Next, on the single bead just above the cross, pray the "Our Father." Remember, Rosary prayers are considered Meditative prayers as opposed to personal prayers. In personal prayer the prayer speaks to God. In meditative prayer we allow God to speak to us through his word and his Spirit.

Our Father

Our Father, Who art in Heaven, hallowed be Thy name; Thy Kingdom come, Thy will be done on earth as it is in Heaven. Give us this day our daily bread; and forgive us our trespasses as we forgive those who trespass against us; and lead us not into temptation, but deliver us from evil.   Amen.

The next cluster on the rosary has 3 beads. With this group of beads, the prayer should recite the "Hail Mary." The prayer should recite 3 Hail Marys while allowing God to speak through his words on the three divine virtues of faith, hope, and love.

Hail Mary

Hail Mary, full of grace, the Lord is with thee, blessed art thou amongst women and blessed is the fruit of thy womb, Jesus. Holy Mary Mother of God, pray for us sinners now and at the hour of our death. Amen.

Repeat this three times.

After the three beads, there is a chain. Hold the bare chain and recite the "Glory be to the Father" prayer.

Glory be to the Father

Glory be to the Father, the Son, and the Holy Spirit.

The next bead is a single bead. Hold this bead in your hand and say the divine mystery of contemplation. For example, if it were a Monday or a Saturday, you would say the first Joyful Mystery, "The Annunciation."

The First Joyful Mystery: The Annunciation of the Angel Gabriel to Mary (Lk 1:26-38)

In the sixth month, the angel Gabriel was sent from God to a town of Galilee called Nazareth, to a virgin betrothed to a man named Joseph, of the house of David, and the virgin's name was Mary. And coming to her, he said, "Hail, favored one! The Lord is with you." But she was greatly troubled at what was said and pondered what sort of greeting this might be. Then the angel said to her, "Do not be afraid, Mary, for you have found favor with God. Behold, you will conceive in your womb and bear a son, and you shall name him Jesus. He will be great and will be called Son of the Most High, and the Lord God will give him the throne of David his father, and he will rule over the house of Jacob forever, and of his kingdom there will be no end." But Mary said to the angel, "How can this be, since I have no relations with a man?" And the angel said to her in reply, "The Holy Spirit will come upon you, and the power of the Most High will overshadow you. Therefore the child to be born will be called holy, the Son of God. And behold, Elizabeth, your relative, has also conceived a son in her old age, and this is the sixth month for her who was called barren; for nothing will be impossible for God." Mary said, "Behold, I am the handmaid of the Lord. May it be done to me according to your word." Then the angel departed from her.

Then you may prayer the "Our Father" prayer for the second time.

Our Father

Our Father, Who art in Heaven, hallowed be Thy name; Thy Kingdom come, Thy will be done on earth as it is in Heaven. Give us this day our daily bread; and forgive us our trespasses as we forgive those who trespass against us; and lead us not into temptation, but deliver us from evil.   Amen.

This brings you to a set of ten beads on the rosary. You should then pray 10 Hail Marys while contemplating the first mystery. The example of The Annunciation is provided above.

Hail Mary

Hail Mary, full of grace, the Lord is with thee, blessed art thou amongst women and blessed is the fruit of thy womb, Jesus. Holy Mary Mother of God, pray for us sinners now and at the hour of our death. Amen.

Repeat this ten times.

After the 10th Hail Mary you will have completed the first of 5 decades. The next section of the rosary, is a single bead. Repeat the "Glory be to the Father."

Glory be to the Father

Glory Be to the Father, the Son, and the Holy Spirit.

Next, on the same bead, pray the "O My Jesus."

O My Jesus

O My Jesus, have mercy on us. Forgive us our sins. Save us from the fires of hell. Take all souls into heaven, especially, those most in need of thy mercy. Amen.

Then, on the same bead, announce the next or second mystery.
For example: if it is Monday and your praying the Joyful
Mysteries, the second Joyful Mystery is The Visitation.

The Second Joyful Mystery: The Visitation of Mary to Elizabeth (Lk 1:39-50)

During those days Mary set out and traveled to the hill
country in haste to a town of Judah, where she entered the
house of Zechariah and greeted Elizabeth. When Elizabeth
heard Mary's greeting, the infant leaped in her womb, and
Elizabeth, filled with the Holy Spirit, cried out in a loud voice
and said, "Most blessed are you among women, and blessed
is the fruit of your womb. And how does this happen to me,
that the mother of my Lord should come to me? For at the
moment the sound of your greeting reached my ears, the
infant in my womb leaped for joy. Blessed are you who
believed that what was spoken to you by the Lord would be
fulfilled." And Mary said: "My soul proclaims the greatness
of the Lord; my spirit rejoices in God my savior. For he has
looked upon his handmaid's lowliness; behold, from now on
will all ages call me blessed. The Mighty One has done great
things for me, and holy is his name. His mercy is from age to
age to those who fear him...."

Next, repeat the "Our Father."

Our Father

Our Father, Who art in Heaven, hallowed be Thy name; Thy
Kingdom come, Thy will be done on earth as it is in Heaven.
Give us this day our daily bread; and forgive us our
trespasses as we forgive those who trespass against us; and
lead us not into temptation, but deliver us from evil.   Amen.

You will now come to the second group of 10 beads. You should pray 10 Hail Marys while contemplating the appropriate mystery.

Hail Mary

Hail Mary, full of grace, the Lord is with thee, blessed art thou amongst women and blessed is the fruit of thy womb, Jesus. Holy Mary Mother of God, pray for us sinners now and at the hour of our death. Amen.

Repeat this ten times.

You may now move on to each mystery, by repeating the cycle as illustrated above. Below are the remaining three joyful mysteries. Generally, The Joyful mysteries are meditated on Monday and Saturdays. The Five Sorrowful Mysteries are mediated on Tuesday & Friday, The Five Glorious Mysteries on Wednesday & Sunday, and The Five Luminous Mysteries on Thursday.

The Third Joyful Mystery: THE BIRTH OF OUR LORD (LK 2:1-14)

In those days a decree went out from Caesar Augustus that the whole world should be enrolled. This was the first enrollment, when Quirinius was governor of Syria. So all went to be enrolled, each to his own town. And Joseph too went up from Galilee from the town of Nazareth to Judea, to the city of David that is called Bethlehem, because he was of the house and family of David, to be enrolled with Mary, his betrothed, who was with child. While they were there, the time came for her to have her child, and she gave birth to her firstborn son. She wrapped him in swaddling clothes and laid him in a manger, because there was no room for them in the inn. Now there were shepherds in that region living in the fields and keeping the night watch over their flock. The angel of the Lord appeared to them and the glory of the Lord shone around them, and they were struck with great fear. The angel said to them, "Do not be afraid; for behold, I proclaim to you good news of great joy that will be for all the people. For today in the city of David a savior has been born for you who is Messiah and Lord. And this will be a sign for you: you will find an infant wrapped in swaddling clothes and lying in a manger." And suddenly there was a multitude of the heavenly host with the angel, praising God and saying: "Glory to God in the highest and on earth peace to those on whom his favor rests."

The Fourth Joyful Mystery: Presentation of Our Lord (Lk 2:22-35)

When the days were completed for their purification according to the law of Moses, they took him up to Jerusalem to present him to the Lord, just as it is written in the law of the Lord, "Every male that opens the womb shall be consecrated to the Lord," and to offer the sacrifice of "a pair of turtledoves or two young pigeons," in accordance with the dictate in the law of the Lord. Now there was a man in Jerusalem whose name was Simeon. This man was righteous and devout, awaiting the consolation of Israel, and the Holy Spirit was upon him. It had been revealed to him by the Holy Spirit that he should not see death before he had seen the Messiah of the Lord. He came in the Spirit into the temple; and when the parents brought in the child Jesus to perform the custom of the law in regard to him, he took him into his arms and blessed God, saying: "Now, Master, you may let your servant go in peace, according to your word, for my eyes have seen your salvation, which you prepared in sight of all the peoples, a light for revelation to the Gentiles, and glory for your people Israel." The child's father and mother were amazed at what was said about him; and Simeon blessed them and said to Mary his mother, "Behold, this child is destined for the fall and rise of many in Israel, and to be a sign that will be contradicted (and you yourself a sword will pierce) so that the thoughts of many hearts may be revealed."

The Fifth Joyful Mystery: The Finding of Our Lord in the Temple (Lk 2:41-52)

Each year his parents went to Jerusalem for the feast of Passover, and when he was twelve years old, they went up according to festival custom. After they had completed its days, as they were returning, the boy Jesus remained behind in Jerusalem, but his parents did not know it. Thinking that he was in the caravan, they journeyed for a day and looked for him among their relatives and acquaintances, but not finding him, they returned to Jerusalem to look for him. After three days they found him in the temple, sitting in the midst of the teachers, listening to them and asking them questions, and all who heard him were astounded at his understanding and his answers. When his parents saw him, they were astonished, and his mother said to him, "Son, why have you done this to us? Your father and I have been looking for you with great anxiety." And he said to them, "Why were you looking for me? Did you not know that I must be in my Father's house?" But they did not understand what he said to them. He went down with them and came to Nazareth, and was obedient to them; and his mother kept all these things in her heart. And Jesus advanced (in) wisdom and age and favor before God and man.

Additional prayers for the rosary are as follows:

LET US PRAY

O God, by the life, death and resurrection of Your only begotten Son, You purchased for us the rewards of eternal life; grant, we beseech You that while meditation on these mysteries of the Holy rosary, we may imitate what they contain and obtain what they promise. Through the same Christ our Lord. Amen.

FATIMA PRAYER

Most Holy Trinity - Father, Son, and Holy Spirit - I adore thee profoundly. I offer Thee the most precious Body, Blood, Soul and Divinity of Jesus Christ, present in all the tabernacles of the world, in reparation for the outrages, sacrileges and indifferences whereby He is offended. And through the infinite merits of His Most Sacred Heart and the Immaculate Heart of Mary, I beg of Thee the conversion of poor sinners.

MEMORARE

Remember, O most gracious Virgin Mary that never was it known that anyone who fled to Your protection, implored Your help, or sought Your intercession was left unaided. Inspired with this confidence, we fly to you, O Virgin of virgins, our Mother. To You we come; before You we stand, sinful and sorrowful. O Mother of the Word Incarnate, despise not our petitions, but in Your mercy, hear and answer us. Amen.

Additional Reading

Bernstein, Carl and Marco Politi. *His Holiness: John Paul II and the Hidden History of Our Time.* New York: Doubleday, 1996.

Berry, Jason and Gerald Renner. *Vows of Silence: The Abuse of Power in the Papacy of John Paul II.* New York: Free Press, 2004.

Dziwisz, Stanislaw (Cardinal). *A Life with Karol: My Forty-Year Friendship with the Man Who Became Pope.* With Gian Franco Swidercoschi. Trans. Adrian J. Walker. New York: Doubleday, 2008.

O'Connor, Garry. *Universal Father: A Life of John Paul II.* New York: Bloomsbury, 2005.

Weigel, George. *Witness to Hope: The Biography of Pope John Paul II.* New York: Cliff Street Books/HarperCollins, 1999.

CPSIA information can be obtained
at www.ICGtesting.com
Printed in the USA
LVHW080217301122
734318LV00014B/1834

9 781491 049662